Peacebound

by

K. G. Lyseng

Ashes of Peace
Book One of the Peacebound Series

ISBN: 9798317684549

Blessed are the peacemakers,

for they shall be called

children of God

Contents

Chapter 1	Ashes in the wind	7
Chapter 2	Shadows at the Edge	13
Chapter 3	The Second Wave	21
Chapter 4	The Golden Hero	27
Chapter 5	A Town Betrayed	37
Chapter 6	A Line in the Ash	43
Chapter 7	After the Flames	51
Chapter 8	The Choice to Stand	61
Chapter 9	The Ashes of Driftwillow	67
Chapter 10	Journey	75
Chapter 11	The Climb	85
Chapter 12	Deep Wisdom	93
Chapter 13	The Truth Beneath the Dust	101
Chapter 14	Hope From Ashes	109
Chapter 15	The Price of Passage	119

Chapter 16	Smoke Over Seabridge	129
Chapter 17	Into the Teeth	139
Chapter 18	Unwelcoming Walls	147
Chapter 19	Where Heroes Fall	159
Chapter 20	Before the Throne	165
Chapter 21	The Broken Crown	171
Chapter 22	Tea and Daggers	181
Chapter 23	Calm Before the Storm	191
Chapter 24	A Whisper Too Loud	203
Chapter 25	Trapped in the Jaws	211
Chapter 26	Defanged	219
Chapter 27	Dawning Hope	229
Epilogue		241

Prologue

Before the kingdoms, before the crowns and the wars, before even the mountains had risen from the sea, there was Shalonai.

Shalonai is not a god made by beast or king. He is not bound to a temple, nor summoned by spell or stone. He is the one true God—the Creator of the heavens and the earth, who breathed life into every creature, and who placed eternity into the heart of even the smallest soul.

Some have forgotten Him. Others twist His name. But those who still walk the path of peace know: all that is good and just flows from Shalonai, the God of mercy, truth, and unshakable light.

Shalonai has many titles.
He is the Shepherd, who leads the lost.
He is the Light, who drives back the darkness.
He is the Creator, from whom all life began.

However, there is one more title that most have forgotten:

The King.

Chapter 1

Ashes in the Wind

Peanut narrowed one eye, aimed, and loosed an arrow.

It sailed wide. Not by much, but enough to send the wooden shaft thudding into a branch just below the target—a red apple swinging gently from a string tied to a tree limb.

Kip cackled. "You call that aiming? That poor branch never stood a chance."

"I'd like to see you do better," Peanut said, brushing her tawny fur from her eyes. Her bow creaked as she handed it to her younger brother. "Here. Show me what a real champion looks like."

Kip snatched the bow and set his feet, tongue poking from the side of his mouth. He pulled the string back with far too much confidence. The arrow wobbled in the air before diving straight into the moss at their feet.

Peanut smirked. "Champion of the ground."

"It slipped," Kip said quickly. "This next one'll get it. For real."

The two squirrels stood in a small clearing just outside Maplebend, their village hidden among the towering maples. Rope bridges stretched between wooden platforms high in the canopy, where homes clung like nests. The summer afternoon bathed everything in warm gold, and birds called lazily overhead.

As Kip prepared another shot, Peanut dropped her teasing. "You hear what Miss Tilda said this morning? About the rumors?"

"That the Claw is marching east?" Kip loosed the second arrow. It flew high and disappeared into the leaves.

Peanut nodded. "Some say they burned the town of Millburrow. Others say the golden army finally pushed them back. No one agrees."

Kip didn't answer. He strung another arrow, took careful aim, and managed to hit the rope. The apple tumbled to the grass.

"Ha!" he shouted. "That counts!"

"Not really," Peanut muttered. She walked over, picked up the apple, and hung it again. She said nothing for a moment, then took a breath and fired.

This time, the arrow clipped the side of the apple, sending it spinning from its string and bouncing along the forest floor.

She should have smiled. But she didn't.

Kip's voice was quieter now. "Do you think... Reese ever saw the Claw?"

Peanut stared at the fallen apple. Reese. Their older brother. He'd left two years ago to join the golden army, to fight for the king, to drive back the darkness clawing at Avareth. He hadn't returned.

"I think he saw more than we can imagine."

They stood in silence, the warmth of the afternoon pressing against their fur, the peace of the woods suddenly feeling thinner than before.

The scent of stew met them before they even reached the door. Miss Tilda's home, nestled in the roots of an ancient maple, looked like it had grown from the earth itself. Herbs hung from every beam, flowers spilled from windowsills, and the front path was lined with stones Kip had painted years ago.

Peanut opened the door slowly.

Miss Tilda glanced up from her pot. Her eyes, wise and soft, narrowed. "Late."

"We were—"

"Practicing," she said, turning back to stir. "I figured. That apple tree's going to develop trust issues."

Kip gave a nervous laugh. "We'll chop extra wood after supper."

"Yes," she said, her voice dry. "You will."

They washed up quickly, and soon the three of them sat around the small wooden table, steam rising from their bowls.

"Did you hear anything new today?" Peanut asked.

Miss Tilda shook her head. "Just whispers. Same as always. Some say the Claw marches east. Others say the king's army finally has them on the run."

Kip perked up. "So maybe it's almost over?"

Miss Tilda didn't smile. "The world doesn't change that quickly. Wars end slowly, like snow melting. And sometimes they freeze again just when you think spring's come."

Peanut stirred her stew. "Why haven't they come here? Maplebend, I mean."

Miss Tilda took a long breath. "Because we're small. Hidden. The war has raged for twenty years across Avareth, and we've stayed out of it—not by strength, but by being unimportant. No king wants this place. No army needs it."

"But if they come now—?"

"Then we'll meet it together," she said gently. "With courage. And with trust in Shalonai."

The name settled over the table like a blanket. Shalonai—the Creator, the Shepherd, the Light. The one Reese had believed in enough to follow into war.

Miss Tilda looked at them both. "You know, I don't expect you to be soldiers. But I do expect you to listen. You don't need to be strong all the time. Shalonai gives rest to the weary, not medals to the brave."

Kip looked down. "Our parents... they didn't get rest."

"No," Miss Tilda said softly. "They got peace. There's a difference."

Peanut swallowed the lump in her throat.

The rest of supper passed in quiet. Miss Tilda hummed as she cleaned. The smell of thyme and firewood wrapped the house in warmth.

The stars were already out when Peanut and Kip left with a small woven basket.

"It's not even that much wood," Kip muttered, kicking a pebble.

"We deserved it," Peanut replied. "We did ditch our chores to go shoot our bow."

"Mine hit the rope."

"Barely."

They laughed, the tension of dinner slipping away. The night air was crisp, but the trees rustled gently overhead, comforting and familiar.

Kip swung the basket idly. "Miss Tilda's worrying too much. The Claw wouldn't waste their time coming here. They've got bigger places to conquer."

"She's just scared. We all are."

Kip hesitated. "Do you think Reese is still alive?"

Peanut looked up at the moonlight slipping through the leaves. "I don't know. But I hope he is. And I hope he never has to come back here."

They reached the edge of the clearing where dry branches lay scattered. Kip bent to pick one up—then froze.

High above, gliding in a lazy circle, was a vulture.

A large one.

Peanut grabbed Kip's arm and yanked him under a thick fern. They crouched, barely breathing.

The vulture didn't cry out. It didn't dive. It simply drifted, its shadow sweeping over the trees like a stain.

Kip whispered, "It saw us. I know it did."

"Stay still."

The bird circled once more, then turned west and vanished beyond the trees.

They didn't move for a long time.

When they finally stood, neither spoke. The branches they were sent to gather lay untouched.

They turned and ran.

They had completely forgotten the firewood.

Chapter 2

Shadows at the Edge

Maplebend was not a grand place. It was a patchwork of rope bridges, hollowed tree homes, and mossy walkways strung between wide-trunked oaks. Most of the town's residents were small creatures—mice, voles, shrews—each with their place in the canopy. And while the world beyond their woods had groaned under war for decades, Maplebend had managed to remain untouched. Forgotten, even. But now, the edges were fraying.

Peanut and Kip were the only squirrels in the village, the last of their kind in these parts, or so Miss Tilda always said. Most others were driven out or lost in battles far from here. It's part of why the kids stand out—Peanut with her scrappy bow and quiver, and Kip with his hand-whittled wooden sword always tucked at his side.

Kip walked along the outer platform near the village edge, just beyond the soup stand where Miss Rindle—a short-legged, broad-shouldered hedgehog with a fierce cooking spoon—usually sold her root stew. Now the stand was closed, and the stew pot was cold.

"You're walking like a soldier already," said Peanut, seated nearby, stringing another arrow.

Kip stopped and leaned on the railing. "Soldiers actually get to fight. We're stuck waiting."

Below them, the preparations continue. Ropes were tightened, walkways reinforced. Boulders and logs were rigged with pulley systems, set to drop if anything tries to climb the trees. Even the youngest were given tasks—carrying messages, sharpening sticks, gathering berries. It was a flurry of anxious motion.

A pair of hares—tall, lean twins with matching scarves hauled up a bundle of thorn-laced vines.

"From the southern slope," one said, panting. "Already cleared. Nothing moving yet."

A grizzled mole with a patch over one eye nodded as he listened. "We'll line the perimeter. No gaps. If they climb, we slice."

Peanut caught fragments of conversations—" ...haven't seen a Claw banner in twenty years this far west..." and "...Varrin's supposed to be camped near Goldhollow. That's only three valleys away."

Kip lit up at the mention. "Did you hear that? Goldhollow! That's less than two days' march. Varrin's close. He'll come. He had to."

Peanut didn't answer. She glanced at the smoke on the horizon. It's thinner than yesterday, but darker. More focused.

They headed back toward Miss Tilda's. Her home was deeper in the branches, built into the largest tree in the grove. The steps creaked as they climbed, and the scent of cinnamon bread lingered faintly in the bark.

Miss Tilda — a short skunk with graying stripes and a limp in her back leg — met them at the door, wrapped in the scent of lavender, tea leaves, and the unmistakable hint of skunk she pretended not to notice (and everyone else politely ignored).

"In. Now," she said, eyes hard. Her apron was dusted with flour, but her claws were out and her voice stern.

Peanut tried, as always, to ease the tension. "We were just checking the western platform. Kip thought he saw a vulture—"

Tilda slammed the door shut. "I don't care if he saw the Shadowed Crown himself. You stay close. Both of you."

Kip dropped his gaze. "They need help. We're not babies, Tilda."

"No," she said. "You're orphans. And I won't lose you too."

The silence after that was thick.

She sighed and walked to the back corner, lifting a woven rug and revealing a trapdoor beneath it. With a grunt, she pulled it open. A cool, earthen scent wafts up.

"This is where we go if they breach the trees. Cellar's stocked. Stone-lined. Hidden under root and soil. You don't leave it until I come get you."

Peanut peeks inside. There were shelves of jars, bundles of herbs, and two wool blankets folded in a corner. Her chest tightened.

"What about you?" she asked.

Miss Tilda places a paw on her shoulder. "I'll be right above you. If I tell you to run, you run."

Kip clenches his jaw. "Why don't you believe we can help?"

Tilda studies him. “Because I know what help costs. And I’ve buried enough brave fools for one lifetime.”

They didn’t argue. Not out loud. But when the house quieted and Miss Tilda busied herself with her mortar and pestle, Peanut caught Kip eyeing his wooden sword like it’s a promise he meant to keep.

Later, on the outer platform, the sun dipped low. Shadows stretched through the forest. The defenders stood at their posts—dozens of creatures, from towering stags with pikes to tiny voles gripping sharpened daggers. Even the village weaver, a quiet ferret with gold-threaded cuffs, held a sling across her shoulder.

A brown-feathered quail from a nearby town, breathless and sweating, hurried up the path. “Saw them,” he panted. “They’re coming through the eastern ridge. Hundreds. Maybe more. Marching under black banners. Claw insignia.”

Gasps rippled through the line.

The one-eyed mole—now clearly the militia leader—gritted his teeth. “Positions. If they reach the bramble wall, signal with the bell vine.”

Peanut and Kip crouched behind the fletching stand, watching. Kip’s breath was quick, but quiet.

"See anything?" Peanut whispered.

He nodded, slowly. "There. On the ridge. Movement. Too many for a hunting party."

Through the trees, just visible in the fading light, rows of dark figures descended the far slope. Vultures with wingblades. Rats in jagged armor. Boars with rusted helmets. Their black banners bear a white talon, painted crudely and flapping in the wind.

Kip whispered, barely audible. “The Claw.”

All across the platform, the defenders froze.

A small bell chimed once. Then again. Then again.

No commands. No speeches. Only silence.

The defenders braced themselves as the Claw poured into the glade, like a shadow came alive.

The forest held its breath.

From high in the canopy, the residents of Maplebend watched as the first wave of the Claw army moved into the glade. There was no war cry, no horns or drums—only the grim sound of armored feet against soil and clawed hands on bark.

The boars came first, snorting and stamping, their rusted armor creaking with each step. Behind them, a line of vulture-knights marched in eerie silence, their feathers dull and eyes gleaming. More followed: weasels with hooked spears, stoats in splintered cuirasses, and rats in tightly packed ranks.

Some of the younger defenders trembled. Others clung tighter to their weapons. Still others stared, stone-faced, at the coming tide.

The first volley came from above—a barrage of sharpened stakes and thorn-studded stones released from the treetop pulleys. Several enemies fell. The boars grunted and reared. But the army did not stop. They climbed.

Hooks were thrown. Ladders were raised. The Claw surged upward, clawing at the trunks like a black tide reaching for the sky.

The defenders roared to life. Arrows rained from the branches. Nets fell. Oil was poured and lit. A stoat screeched as he plummeted in flames. A vulture was caught mid-flight by a thrown javelin, its wings snapping as it spiraled down.

The bramble wall held—for a moment.

Then a section was blasted open by a crude bomb—a keg of pitch rolled in and lit. The explosion splintered bark and blew open a path. Through it charged a squad of armored rats, shrieking battle cries.

The outer platforms were the first to fall. The defenders fought fiercely, but they were outnumbered. Miss Rindle, swinging her iron ladle, took down two attackers before she was struck from behind and crumpled. One of the hares fell protecting the other, who dragged him back into the inner branches.

The defenders retreated, platform by platform, deeper into the trees. Fires caught. Ropes burned. Some bridges collapsed under the weight of fleeing villagers. The canopy became a battlefield of smoke and cries.

At Miss Tilda's, the trapdoor was closed. The house shook from distant blasts. Below, in the root cellar, Peanut and Kip sat in silence, listening.

Kip gripped his wooden sword so tightly his paw trembled. Peanut leaned close, eyes fixed upward. Another explosion. Shouts. Then the unmistakable creak of the front door upstairs.

Voices. Heavy footfalls.

And then—Miss Tilda, shouting. A crash. The sound of a struggle. A cry.

Peanut leapt to her feet.

"Stay," Kip whispered.

But she was already moving. She climbed the ladder and eased the trapdoor open a crack. Smoke curled in. She saw movement—shadows, claws, a rat rifling through cupboards. And Miss Tilda, pinned beneath a broken shelf, blood at her temple.

Peanut's breath caught. She shut the trapdoor softly.

Kip stared at her. "Is she—?"

"We have to help her," Peanut said. Kip swallowed, then nodded. He pulled the wooden sword from his belt. Together, they pushed open the trapdoor and stepped into the burning night.

The room was chaotic. Flames licked the rafters. The rat had his back to them, too busy ransacking a cabinet to notice. Peanut moved first. She grabbed the leg of a stool and hurled it. It smashed against the wall beside the rat, who snarled and spun, just as Kip charged.

The wooden sword cracked across the rat's snout. He howled and lunged, claws slashing, but Kip ducked beneath the swing. Peanut dived in, stabbing with an arrowhead gripped in her paw.

The rat stumbled back, bleeding. He hissed, then bolted out the door and vanished into the smoke.

"Kip, the shelf!" Peanut shouted.

Together, they lifted the broken shelf off Miss Tilda.

She groaned. "Still here," she muttered. "I'm not that easy to—" She tried to rise, but her leg gave out.

"Stay down," Peanut said. "We'll get you somewhere safe."

Miss Tilda grabbed Peanut's arm, eyes sharp despite the pain. "Others out there. Help them first. Go."

Peanut hesitated.

"Now!" the skunk growled.

They dragged her to the trapdoor and lowered her into the cellar. Kip handed her a jar of salve and a small dagger.

"You better still be here when we get back," he said.

Tilda gave him a weak smile. "Go be brave, little fools."

They rushed outside into the night.

The canopy was ablaze. Platforms sagged and burned. Creatures fled across the bridges—some wounded, some carrying others. A weasel cub cried out from a collapsed walkway, pinned beneath a broken beam.

"There!" Peanut yelled.

She sprinted ahead while Kip circled wide, using a back path to approach from the other side. The cub was a mess of fur and blood, his leg trapped. Peanut grabbed a fallen spear and wedged it beneath the beam. "On three!" she shouted.

Kip nodded, adding his weight to the lever. "One... two... three!"

The beam lifted just enough. Peanut dragged the cub free. A roar split the air. A hulking badger in Claw colors barreled toward them, mace raised. Peanut threw herself over the cub.

A blur of movement—a wildcat from Maplebend's guard—slammed into the badger. They tumbled, claws and fury.

"Go!" the cat yelled.

Kip and Peanut ran, the cub between them.

Chapter 3

The Second Wave

The night air was thick with smoke and panic.

Peanut and Kip darted between burning walkways, hauling the weasel cub to a safe cluster of defenders under a scorched platform. The cub's mother, a wiry weasel with singed whiskers, clasped the child with tears in her eyes.

"You saved him," she whispered, brushing soot from Peanut's cheek. "Bless you."

There was no time for thanks. Another horn blew to the north. A tremor rolled through the wooden supports beneath their feet. Kip grabbed Peanut's paw. "More are coming."

Around them, the defenders of Maplebend rallied. Foxes with slings, rabbits with bows, and a massive badger with a cracked shield formed a ragged line at the edge of the burning village. Some still wore aprons or sleeping clothes. Others had armor cobbled together from tin or bark. But all wore the same expression: fear hardened into resolve.

"Form up!" called a lynx captain, his left ear torn and still bleeding. "Hold the northern bridges! Don't let them break the line!"

Peanut and Kip joined a trio of younger fighters—a small mole with a bandaged paw, a hedgehog clutching a spear too long for him, and a quiet raccoon who didn't speak but stood firm. Together, they fell into step, running toward the line.

Each platform was a battlefield. Arrows zipped past their heads. Smoke stung their eyes. Every tree, every bridge, every rope was a defense line. They passed familiar shops now scorched and broken—the baker's ledge collapsed, the apothecary's vines on fire.

A vulture dived overhead, claws outstretched. Peanut ducked just in time, feeling the gust of its wings. A bluejay—an elder from the grain loft—brought the bird down with a thrown axe.

The ground beneath them shuddered again. Kip glanced north.

"Is that... thunder?"

It wasn't.

"Enemy scouts sighted nearby! Possible raiding force approaching! All hands prepare!"

Kip ran toward the smithy with another blade, only to find the blacksmith too busy fitting armor plates to listen. Peanut was pulled from the kitchens to help transport bandages to the infirmary tent.

Neither of them was handed a weapon. Neither was called to the front.

But both watched.

The King rode out with a vanguard. The rest of the camp stayed on alert for hours—watching the trees, guarding the road, preparing for attack.

It never came.

The enemy vanished like smoke.

When Varrin returned, his armor dusted with travel but his eyes sharp, he spoke briefly with his commanders. As he passed through the camp, his gaze fell on the two squirrels.

He slowed, dismounted.

"You were both in the supply lines today?" he asked, voice low but clear.

They nodded, standing straight.

"Good," he said. "A soldier's strength is more than what they carry in their paws. It is how they carry the burden. You both carried yours well."

Peanut felt her chest lift. Kip's tail curled upright with pride.

It wasn't battle. It wasn't glory.

But it was something.

From that night on, things changed—not dramatically, but enough. One of the sword trainers began giving Kip five minutes of real practice after drills, showing him how to stand, how to block. Peanut was assigned to help with ration inventory, where she learned to calculate supply needs for an entire unit.

They were still cooks, still couriers.

But they were also being watched. And slowly, they were being shaped.

Chapter 5

A Town Betrayed

The wind had carried the scent of smoke long before the fires began.

Peanut stood on a ridge overlooking the valley below, her heart twisting at the sight. The village of Sunridge lay quiet, its wooden walls barely fortified, its rooftops glowing golden in the afternoon sun. She recognized the buildings—the watchtower near the well, the grain mill by the river. They had passed through this town just a season ago with Miss Tilda. She remembered sharing honeycakes with the baker's son and trading nuts with a rabbit girl who had a pet cricket.

Now, Sunridge was to be a battlefield.

Behind her, the golden army moved in organized waves—armor glinting, spears swaying. The banners of King Varrin whipped in the wind like tongues of fire. Peanut clutched her arms tightly around her chest. She hadn't been given armor or even a job today. She had been told to stay out of the way. She didn't feel like a soldier. She felt like a child watching a nightmare unfold.

"Kip!" she called, spotting him among a group of soldiers by the edge of camp. He was being handed something—a helmet.

He ran to her, beaming.

"Peanut! Guess what? They picked me! I'm marching with the front line!"

"What?" she whispered, shocked. "You're... fighting?"

Kip nodded proudly. "A few of the older soldiers said I shouldn't be running errands anymore. Said I was ready. They even gave me a helmet! Can you believe that?"

Her eyes dropped to the weapon at his side—a polished short sword. Real. Heavy. Deadly.

"You can't be serious."

He looked hurt. "Why not? This town chose the Claw. They knew what they were doing. And besides... they said this won't even be a real fight. Sunridge doesn't stand a chance. I'm not in any danger."

"That's not the point!" she snapped. "You know this town, Kip! We both did! They're just scared. Like Maplebend was. Like we were!"

"Yeah, but we chose to fight. They chose to side with monsters."

Peanut stared at him, the disbelief cutting deeper than she expected. "Maybe they didn't choose anything. Maybe they were just afraid. Maybe that vulture you saw with the mayor was a threat, not a guest. You ever think about that?"

Kip looked away. "I don't know. Maybe. But I'm part of the army now. And when you're in the army, you follow orders."

Her voice dropped to a growl. "Even if those orders were wrong?"

He didn't answer.

She turned her back on him. "Go fight your battle, then."

He flinched, hurt flashing across his face. "Peanut—"

She was already walking away.

The sun began to dip low, casting long shadows over the field. The signal horn sounded once—short and sharp. Kip stood in formation, surrounded by warriors towering over him. His helmet sat awkwardly on his head, the sword heavy in his paws. His heart beat faster than it ever had.

"Stay close to your line," said a fox soldier beside him. "Just move forward and keep your eyes open. Today's easy. They won't even fight back."

Kip nodded, but his mouth was dry.

Ahead, the village gates were shut, but no defenders stood atop the walls. No arrows flew. No sound but the flags whipping in the breeze. He didn't feel like a hero. He felt like a stormcloud, ready to rain destruction on people who had done nothing to him.

Behind the lines, unseen and unheard, Peanut crept after the army. She moved silently between carts and shadows, her small size a gift in the bustle of preparation. She didn't know what she was going to do. She just knew she couldn't let Kip march into that town.

He was her brother. Her family. And she would not let this war take him too.

The horn sounded a second time.

Kip took a step forward.

So did Peanut.

The battle had begun.

Sunridge never stood a chance.

The town had pulled together a small defense—mostly farmers with pitchforks and a few retired guards gripping old, rusty swords. They lined the narrow streets and rooftops, hoping the town's familiar layout might help them. But as King Varrin's golden army reached the top of the ridge and began marching down, the truth became clear: Sunridge was not ready for war.

The golden army moved like a wave—steady and strong. Shields locked together. Rows straight. Archers ready. Sunridge's weak walls fell quickly. Doors broke under heavy battering rams. The clash of metal drowned out cries for help. It wasn't a real fight. It was a storm. And Sunridge was just a dry leaf caught in the wind.

Some townsfolk tried to be brave. An old hedgehog used a spear to trip a soldier before he was surrounded. Three young raccoons threw stones from a rooftop, but ran when arrows flew back. A badger blacksmith stood in front of his forge with a hammer, but was pulled away by soldiers. These small moments of courage burned like candles—and each one went out too soon.

The vulture that had stood next to the mayor disappeared when the fighting started. No one knew if it flew back to the Claw or simply ran away. All that remained was smoke, fear, and surrender.

The golden army moved through the town slowly and calmly. By sunset, the defenders were beaten. The town square was crowded with those who hadn't run fast enough.

Kip marched with the army, sword in hand, heart racing with excitement and fear. The path into Sunridge was strangely quiet—no guards, no warning shouts. The gates had been broken down without a fight. The soldiers entered in rows, their armor shining in the fading sunlight.

For a moment, Kip felt swept up in it all—the steady beat of boots, the flash of flags, the feeling of being part of something big. He had finally made it. This was his first battle. This was the start of his story.

He didn't notice the silence. Not until it ended.

A wooden platform stood in the town square. On it, King Varrin stood tall, his golden armor shining, his red cape blowing in the breeze. The townspeople who hadn't escaped were gathered in the square, scared and unsure. Children hugged their mothers. Old animals sat on the ground, shaking. Kip saw familiar faces—a baker, a trader, a girl with a ribbon tied behind her ears.

Varrin raised his paw. The army went quiet. His voice rang out, loud and strong:

"This town had a choice. A choice to stand with justice, or to kneel to evil. And they chose the enemy."

Worried whispers spread through the crowd. Kip held his breath.

"By joining the Claw," Varrin said, "they have become the Claw. And so, like the Claw, they must fall."

The crowd stood still.

Then Varrin shouted, "Take everything. Burn what you can't carry. Leave no trace of traitors."

For a moment, Kip couldn't move. He stood frozen in the middle of the square as soldiers around him began to cheer. Doors were kicked open. Windows smashed. Fires lit. Screams rose into the sky.

Peanut heard the last part of the speech from just outside the town walls. Her breath caught in her throat. She watched in horror as the village burst into chaos. Soldiers rushed into houses, pulling out families. Fires spread like sickness. The people of Sunridge tried to run, but there was nowhere to go.

She stumbled forward, slipping past soldiers and smoke, shouting Kip's name. But her voice was swallowed by the noise.

A cart full of vegetables had been flipped over, crushed by boots. A group of foxes stormed into a tailor's shop. A young badger, no older than five, cried behind the town well.

Then she saw him.

Kip stood still near the edge of the square, sword hanging at his side. He stared at the bakery as flames swallowed it. Not far away, a mother dropped to her knees, begging someone—anyone—to protect her children.

He wasn't smiling anymore.

Peanut pushed through the crowd of soldiers and smoke, grabbed his arm.

"Kip!"

He turned to her, surprised. His face was pale under the helmet.

"Peanut... this isn't... this wasn't what I thought it would be..."

Tears ran down her face—not from the smoke, but from anger. "We have to stop this. We have to do something."

Behind them, Sunridge burned. The cries of scared families rose louder than any trumpet. Kip looked at his sword—not with pride, but with shame.

He gave a small nod.

They turned toward the fire. Together.

They pushed through the smoke, keeping low as flames snapped overhead. The heat stung their eyes and filled their noses with the bitter stench of ash. Around them, chaos still roared—shouts, crashes, the endless crackle of fire devouring wood and cloth.

Then they saw him.

King Varrin strode through the burning streets like a shadow carved from gold. His armor still gleamed, but it no longer looked bright or noble. It looked sharp. Dangerous. His mane whipped in the wind, and his eyes—once warm with courage—burned with fury.

He didn't shout commands now. He didn't wave his sword. He walked slowly, calmly, as if the fire and screams were nothing more than background noise. A soldier approached to speak with him, but Varrin barely looked at him—just pointed, and the soldier ran off.

The admiration they'd once felt—that rush of awe when Varrin saved Maplebend, when he lifted his shining sword and promised to end the war—it crumbled. The lion that stood before them now was not a savior. He was a storm, full of power, yes—but also full of rage. Peanut stepped back. Kip's paw shook. They were afraid of him, because they finally saw what he could do with that strength.

Chapter 6

A Line in the Ash

The fire still smoldered behind them.

Peanut and Kip walked straight through the wreckage of Sunridge past broken carts, burned homes, and the quiet cries of survivors. The golden flags still flew above the ruins, bright and clean against the dark, smoky sky. But nothing about this felt like a victory.

They found King Varrin on a small hill near the edge of town, speaking with his captains beside a map nailed to a broken fence. He looked up as the two squirrels approached, his face hard to read.

Peanut stepped forward first, her voice shaking with anger. "That wasn't a battle. That was a slaughter."

Varrin watched her. "It was a message. One the rest of the land will understand."

"You destroyed a town," Kip said, his voice quieter but just as steady. "Those people weren't helping the Claw. They were scared. Just like we were in Maplebend."

Varrin let out a long breath and placed his paws behind his back. "And what would you have had me do? Leave them alone? Let them hide spies? Let the Claw grow stronger while we show kindness to those too afraid to choose a side?"

Peanut clenched her fists. "You could've talked to them. Helped them. Give them time. You didn't even try."

The lion king's mane shifted gently in the breeze. "I did try. I gave their leaders a choice. They made it."

"With a vulture standing behind them," Peanut snapped. "You saw it. You knew they were scared."

Varrin looked away. "Fear is part of this war. I won't let it rule me. I will defeat it."

Kip stepped beside his sister. "This isn't what we joined for. We thought you were fighting for peace."

"So did I," Varrin said quietly. "Twenty years ago. But peace doesn't come to those who wait. It comes to those who end the war."

Peanut stared at him, surprised by how cold his voice sounded. "At what cost?"

The lion turned fully to face them. His golden eyes burned with fire. "I chose you because I believed you had the courage to fight for something better. But if you can't handle what must be done... maybe I chose wrong."

Silence fell between them.

Peanut spoke first. "Then maybe we made a mistake too."

Varrin nodded once. "You're free to go."

Peanut narrowed her eyes. "Just like that?"

"You came by choice. You may leave the same way."

She held his gaze for a moment, then turned. Kip followed. They walked away—past the burned homes, the sad townsfolk, the cheering soldiers. Each step felt heavier than the last.

Behind them, Varrin didn't move.

A soldier stepped up beside him, armor shining. "Should we follow them, sire?"

Varrin didn't take his eyes off the horizon. "Take care of it. Quietly."

The soldier nodded and slipped into the smoke.

Down the hill, Peanut and Kip broke into a run. They didn't know where they were going, only that they had to get far away—fast.

The night was darker than any they had ever known.

Peanut and Kip had barely made it beyond the edge of the burned forest when they heard it—the crunch of boots behind them, soft at first, then louder. Closer.

"They're following us," Kip whispered.

Peanut pulled him behind a fallen tree. "I know."

Another snap. Twigs cracking. Shadows moved through the dark. Bits of golden armor caught the faint glow of moonlight.

"We should've run farther," Kip muttered, paw gripping the handle of his dull training sword.

"There wasn't time. We're still too close."

They turned and ran again—through tall grass and deeper into the woods. But no matter how far they went, the soldiers stayed just behind, closing the gap.

At last, they reached a small stream. The water bubbled softly in the quiet night. Across the water, two golden-armored soldiers stepped into view.

"We gave you a chance to leave," one of them said, voice calm but cold. "But you had to speak to the king."

"We're just kids!" Kip shouted.

"Exactly," said the second soldier. "No one will miss you."

The two moved forward.

Peanut grabbed a broken branch, her eyes wide with fear. Kip raised his sword, shaking. They stood together, side by side, ready to fight—even if it wouldn't help.

The soldiers jumped.

A blur shot past Peanut's eyes.

The first soldier fell with a grunt, tripped by a spinning flash of brown fur and water-slick speed. An otter, fast and lean, darted between the attackers like lightning.

The second soldier turned to strike, but a golden retriever leapt from the bushes, crashing into him and knocking them both to the ground.

Then a huge shape stepped from the shadows—quiet and steady. An elephant, calm and strong, entered the clearing. With one smooth swing of his trunk, he slammed both soldiers into a tree.

Peanut and Kip stood frozen.

The otter turned, brushing a leaf off her whiskers. "That was close."

The dog rolled to his paws, rubbing his shoulder. "Told you they'd send someone after them."

The elephant nodded. "Let's move. Others might be coming."

Peanut blinked. "Who... who are you?"

The otter grinned. "Friends. The kind that don't burn towns."

The dog gave a short laugh. "And the kind that don't think kids should be hunted for telling the truth."

Kip stepped forward. "Why... why did you help us?"

The elephant finally spoke. His deep voice was calm and kind. "Because someone needs to. Come with us. You're not safe here."

Peanut paused, then nodded. She and Kip followed the strangers into the woods—away from the fire, away from the army, and away from the world they thought they knew.

The forest around them hummed softly in the twilight. The whisper of leaves and the soft crackle of twigs underfoot mixed with the distant calls of night birds. Peanut and Kip hurried along a narrow path, the weight of their close escape still pressing on their chests. Ahead, three figures led the way—the little otter Orin, the steady elephant Malik, and the cheerful golden retriever Victor. Their steps were sure and steady, each one pulling the children farther from danger.

Behind them trotted Victor, his bright eyes scanning the shadows. He moved like a born scout—ears twitching, nose sniffing, always alert for signs that someone might still be chasing them. Victor was their lookout, guarding them from the darkness just beyond the trees.

The path opened into a small clearing hidden beneath tall oaks and thick ferns. A loose circle of tents made of canvas and patched leather surrounded a warm fire. Around it, a few animals sat or stood, their faces showing both tiredness and strength. The fire's flickering light gave the place a fragile feeling of safety in a world torn by war.

Orin slowed and stopped near the fire, motioning for Peanut and Kip to come closer. Her sleek fur shimmered in the firelight, and her eyes were sharp but kind.

"This is the Peacebound," she said quietly, her voice calm and steady. "You're safe here, with those who won't just stand by and watch the war destroy everything."

Peanut and Kip looked at each other, then stepped forward. Malik's huge shape stood beside the fire like a strong wall, his gentle eyes full of quiet strength. Victor lounged nearby with a lopsided grin, his tail thumping the ground. He tossed a pinecone in the air and caught it in his mouth before giving the kids a playful wink.

Orin gestured to the circle. "We're a small group, but we carry a heavy purpose. We've fought in different ways—some with swords, some with words—but all with the same goal: to end this war."

She paused, then went on. "This war has lasted twenty years. Twenty years of fire and loss. It started with the hope of stopping cruelty and bringing peace. But somewhere along the way, the war became its own monster."

Malik's deep voice rumbled in agreement. "The war feeds on itself, growing stronger after every battle. One side takes a town, then loses it again. It just keeps going, leaving behind nothing but sadness."

Victor's voice turned serious. "I used to think war was all flags and cheering. Turns out it's mostly mud, fire, and graves." He gave a bitter chuckle. "Guess that's what happens when you grow up too fast."

Orin's gaze grew sharper. "It's a beast with no master. Both armies are stuck in its teeth. They don't fight for justice anymore. They fight just to keep going."

She looked straight at Peanut and Kip. "You joined King Varrin's army hoping to help. So did many others. But this war isn't about good and evil anymore. It's about surviving—and that survival comes at a terrible cost."

Peanut's voice trembled. "But how can that be right? All the pain, all the fear... It feels like the same kind of cruelty we were supposed to stop."
Orin nodded. "It is the same. Sometimes the worst enemy wears a crown, not claws."

Malik leaned forward. "That's why we joined the Peacebound. We don't answer to kings or generals. We fight for the ones caught in the middle—for families, for kids like you, for a future without fear."

Victor leaned back, staring into the fire. "We've all lost someone. I joke a lot, but that's just so I don't forget what I've lost. We're here because we still believe in love, laughter—and peace."

Orin's voice softened, though it stayed strong. "We work in secret, finding others who are done with fighting. We don't think peace will come from more battles. It will come from courage—the courage to stand together and break the cycle of hate."

Peanut felt something stir inside her. Hope. Though doubt still tugged at the edges. "It feels too big. How can we stop something that's been going on for so long?"

Orin smiled gently, a spark of warmth in her eyes. "It won't be easy. The road will be long, and there will be loss. But peace is worth every step."

Malik nodded. "Every victory starts with one choice—to do what's right, even when it's hard."

Victor's voice dropped to a whisper. "We fight for the ones who can't anymore... and maybe make someone laugh along the way."

Peanut looked at Kip, then back to Orin. "We want to help. We want to stop this."

Chapter 7

After the Flames

The dawn light crept slowly over the ridge as the last echoes of King Varrin's golden army faded into the distance. From their hidden place among the thick trees, Peanut, Kip, and the rest of the Peacebound watched in silence.

Sunridge—once a lively town in the valley—was now little more than smoking ruins. Smoke still rose from broken rooftops, and the sharp smell of burnt wood hung heavy in the air. The fields that had fed the village for years were flattened and bare.

Orin stood beside the children, her sharp eyes watching the last of the soldiers disappear. "They're gone," she said softly. "For now."

Victor shifted his weight, still alert despite the calm. "No scouts or stragglers. We have a small window before someone else comes."

Malik, the huge elephant, gave a slow nod. "Then let's move."

The group slipped down the hill into the ruined town. The streets were strangely quiet, except for the crackle of dying fires and the soft cries of those who had survived.

Peanut's heart tightened as she saw the damage up close. Homes were turned to piles of ash. A cart lay flipped over, its goods ruined. Doors hung crooked on broken frames. But the worst part was the faces—tired, scared, and hopeless.

A small group of villagers huddled near the remains of the town square. Among them were children wrapped in thin blankets, elders leaning on shaky arms, and mothers holding crying babies.

Kip stepped forward, his voice soft. "We're here to help. You're safe now."

One of the survivors, a tired badger woman, looked up with hollow eyes. "Safe? After what they did? How can anyone be safe when the golden army burns everything?"

Orin knelt beside her. "We're Peacebound. We're here to protect you and fight for an end to this war."

The woman's eyes flickered with a tiny spark of hope, but fear quickly covered it. "We've lost so much..."

"We know," Orin said gently, placing a paw on her shoulder. "That's why we must move quickly."

Malik and Victor began helping the survivors, gathering what little they had left. The Peacebound shared food and water from their packs and helped with cuts, bruises, and broken hearts.

Peanut guided a few children to a safer spot behind a strong stone wall, whispering kind words to calm their nerves. Kip stayed with the adults, listening to their stories and asking who was missing or where others might have fled.

The secret home of the Peacebound, called The Hollow, was hidden deep in the nearby forest—a quiet place of caves and shelters, untouched by the armies and safe from harm. It was where they brought those in need, a place to rest, heal, and hope again.

Orin called the survivors together. "We'll guide you to The Hollow. It's hidden from the world, but there you'll be safe. You'll have a chance to rebuild." A soft wave of hope passed through the crowd.

Peanut looked at Kip. Both of them felt the pain of what had happened—but also something else. A spark. A quiet, brave feeling that maybe, just maybe, peace was still possible.

As the group got ready to leave, Orin looked back at the ruined town. "Sunridge will become a memory," she said. "But this war will not win. Not while we still stand."

Together, the Peacebound and the survivors stepped into the shadowed forest, leaving the ashes behind—carrying the hope of a better future.

The journey took most of the day.

Through winding forest paths and sunny clearings, the Peacebound led the tired survivors deeper into the woods than Peanut and Kip had ever gone. Malik carried the smallest children on his broad back, while Victor stayed at the back, always watching for anyone who might follow.

The trees grew thicker, their leafy roof above blocking out most of the sunlight. The air grew cooler and quieter—like the forest was holding its breath.

At the front of the line, Orin moved quickly and confidently, weaving through bushes and around rocks like she was following a map no one else could see.

At last, the path opened into a narrow gap between two steep hills. At the end stood a tree—or what was left of one. It must have been huge once, towering high over the forest. Now, it stood like a giant skeleton. Its trunk was black and hollow, its twisted branches reaching out like claws.

Peanut and Kip slowed down as they neared it. The tree looked old and tired, its bark rough and cracked like dried mud. But Orin didn't stop. She walked straight into the hollow trunk.

Malik turned to the others. "Welcome," he said quietly. "You've reached the Hollow."

Peanut and Kip looked at each other with wide eyes before following the others inside. At first, it was dark. Then, a torch lit up ahead. Then another. Then more, one by one, lighting a sloped ramp that led down into the ground. They walked down.

As they reached the bottom, the darkness faded and gave way to light—and the stillness turned into life.

The Hollow was not just a cave. It was a city, built under the roots of the dead tree, shaped into tunnels and wide rooms. Warm light glowed from lanterns hanging on ropes. Rope bridges stretched over open spaces. Stalls buzzed with animals selling bread, fruit, herbs, and cloth. Children ran between shops and homes, their laughter bouncing off the walls.

Peanut's mouth dropped open. Kip blinked in amazement.

"This was... all under the tree?" Peanut whispered.

Victor chuckled. "Most folks react like that. We've been building it for years."

Kip pointed to a large square, where some animals played happy music on wooden instruments. "It's like a real town."

"It is a real town," Orin said, stepping beside them. "It's a place where the war can't reach. Not here."

Peanut looked around—then suddenly stopped. "Kip... look."

Across the square, a vulture in a dark cloak was buying vegetables from a mouse. Nearby, a boar with chipped tusks was fixing a broken cart. On a bridge above, an eagle sat beside a lion, laughing as they shared a drink. A panther lay near a library, eyes closed and calm.

All of them. Together. Peaceful.

"But... they're..." Kip tried to find the words. "That's the Claw army. And those—those are Varrin's soldiers. How are they—?"

"They were," Orin said softly. "Some still carry their scars. But many came here to stop fighting. To choose something better."

Peanut frowned. "But I thought... the Claw were the bad ones. And Varrin's army were the good ones."

Orin sighed. "That's what they want you to think. But the truth is harder. More messy. War changes everyone. It hurts everyone. And once it starts... it grows on its own. That's why this place exists."

Malik stepped forward, his voice deep and calm. "We didn't judge here. Not by kind. Not by army. Only by actions. If someone truly wanted peace—if they were ready to let go of hate—they were welcome."

Victor added, "We had rules, of course. No fighting. No flags. Everyone was equal."

Peanut looked again at the mix of animals—hawks flying above, goats growing gardens, a fox reading to a circle of young ones. It felt impossible. And yet... it was real.

"It's like a dream," she said softly.

"It's hope," Orin replied. "It's what the world could be—if we stopped letting others choose our enemies."

Kip looked up at the huge stone walls, the deep tunnels, the years of work it must have taken to build it. "But... this must have taken forever. How did you hide it?"

Victor grinned. "That's Peacebound business."

Malik rolled his eyes. "Which means he won't tell you."

They all laughed, and for the first time in days, Peanut and Kip felt something loosen in their chests. A heavy feeling started to lift.

Not everything was lost.

That night, the children were given a small sleeping nook carved into the trunk wall. As they snuggled into the soft moss bed, Peanut looked out at the warm lights of the Hollow.

"We're really here," she whispered. "Somewhere safe."

Kip nodded sleepily. "Maybe… maybe this is where we're supposed to be."

But deep down, both knew their journey wasn't finished. Not yet.

The war still burned beyond the trees.

And the Hollow—for all its wonder—would need protecting.

Just as that thought settled in Peanut's heart, a quiet noise stirred in the square below their room. Some Peacebound members were gathering near the food carts, giving out supplies to the newest arrivals. Some of the children were crying, holding on tight to family. Mothers rocked babies. The hurt leaned on each other, wrapped in rough bandages.

Among them walked a fox.

His fur was light red, with silver stripes on his face and tail. He wore no armor, no shiny cloak, no crown. Just a plain brown robe with worn edges and a wooden walking stick that tapped gently as he walked. But every animal he passed looked at him with quiet respect—not fear, not power, but something gentler. Trust.

He stopped to help an old badger sit, giving her his blanket. He shared food with a group of young hares. When a squirrel kit dropped his water jug, the fox bent down slowly, picked it up, and said something kind that made the child smile through tears.

Orin appeared beside Peanut and Kip, watching the fox from above.

"That's Kazik," she said softly. "The heart of the Peacebound."

Peanut's eyes grew wide. "That's your leader?"

"He's… not what I expected," Kip said. "He looks… normal."

Orin smiled. "Exactly. He's not praised like Varrin. Not feared like Varnack. But he's done more good than either of them ever will."

They watched as Kazik picked up a basket of bread and carried it to a family in the corner. He sat down, letting a young one curl up in his lap.

A moment later, Orin waved for them to come. "Come on. He wants to meet you."

They hesitated—but followed.

When they reached him, Kazik looked up and gave a warm, tired smile. His eyes were dark brown—the kind that saw all the way through you.

"These must be our brave travelers," he said. His voice was soft, but strong underneath—like tree roots under the dirt.

"This is Peanut and Kip," Orin said. "They've already seen more pain than most."

Kazik nodded slowly. "Then they already understand the world better than many grownups do."

He offered them a seat on a low bench. They sat, unsure what to say.

Kazik looked at them. "Tell me... what do you think will end this war?"

Kip leaned forward. "The strongest army. When one side wins for real—maybe Peacebound, or maybe Varrin—then the other has to stop. Right?"

Kazik didn't answer. He turned to Peanut.

Peanut lowered her eyes. "I... I don't think it can end. Not really. Everyone's already too hurt. Too angry. It just keeps going."

Kazik stayed quiet for a moment, watching them both. Then he smiled—not proud, not sad, but like someone who had heard every answer before.

Kip frowned. "What? What do you think will end it?"

Kazik stood slowly, his joints popping, and reached out a paw. He gently touched each of their heads.

Then he said, "The world teaches war. It tells the strong to crush, the loud to lead, and the angry to win. But the Creator says something else. He says, 'Blessed are the peacemakers, for they will be called children of Shalonai.'"

He looked around the fire, meeting the eyes of every creature nearby.

"Not peacekeepers. Not the ones who avoid pain or run from hard truth. Shalonai blesses the peacemakers. The ones who step into hurt places and say, 'Enough.' The ones who show mercy, even when revenge would be easier. The ones who rebuild what hate has burned."

His eyes shimmered with old memories.

"Peace doesn't mean quiet. It means healing. It means speaking truth. Forgiving what others say can't be forgiven. Bringing light to the places the world gave up on. It's the harder road—but it's the Creator's road. And if we walk it—even limping, even hurting—He walks with us."

Then he added, "Justice without mercy is like a sword without a handle. You might swing it—but you won't be able to hold on."

Without another word, Kazik walked away—back into the crowd, where a wounded hedgehog was trying to stand.

They watched him go.

Peanut blinked. "Did we say something wrong?"

Orin shook her head. "No. He just doesn't waste words. Kazik believes the best answers are the ones you find yourself."

Kip looked down at the Hollow—this quiet town of peace, hidden under a world of war—and wondered what kind of answer might finally be strong enough to stop it all.

Their new home was little more than a carved-out nook tucked into the roots of the Hollow's massive central tree. The walls were rounded, smooth, and warm to the touch, and the earthy smell of dirt and moss hung in the air. A simple lantern glowed dimly from a hook above their sleeping mats, casting long shadows that danced across the curved ceiling.

It was quiet—so quiet that Peanut could hear the distant drip of water, the occasional laughter from others down the hall, and the soft rustle of her brother turning over beside her.

She stared up at the root-covered ceiling, hands behind her head, eyes wide even though she felt so tired.

Kip broke the silence first. "It's weird, isn't it?"

Peanut turned her head toward him. "What is?"

"Being safe. Like, actually safe." He let out a breath. "I keep waiting for someone to shout. Or for fire. Or marching."

She nodded slowly. "I know. I still hear it in my head—the battle. The screaming. The way Sunridge burned." She swallowed. "I keep thinking about

Mom and Dad. What they'd say if they saw all this. The Peacebound. The Hollow."

Kip was quiet for a moment. "I think they'd like it here."

Peanut smiled a little. "Yeah. I think so too."

They lay there in silence for a while longer. The lantern's light started to flicker lower as the oil burned away. Kip rolled onto his side, facing her. "Do you think we'll stay?"

Peanut shrugged. "I don't know. We've been running for so long, it's hard to think about... stopping. But it feels different here. Like... we're not just hiding anymore. We're part of something."

Kip pulled the blanket tighter over himself. "The Peacebound are different. Not like Varrin's army. Not like the Claw. They don't shout orders or punish you for being weak. They help people. Even the ones they're supposed to hate."

Peanut thought of the vultures she had seen building new shelters. Of the lion cub playing tag with a wild boar in the Hollow's open court.

"That part still doesn't feel real," she admitted. "Eagles, vultures, foxes, panthers—side by side. No armor. No yelling."

"No walls between them," Kip said.

Peanut smiled. "Kazik... he's different too."

Kip nodded quickly. "He's nothing like Varrin. Or Varnak. They're like statues on a mountain, always above everyone. But Kazik—he's just... there. Like the Hollow itself."

"He helped that little shrew family earlier," Peanut said, eyes thoughtful. "He carried their bags himself. No guards. No big speech. Just helped."

"I don't get it," Kip said softly. "He's the leader, right? Why would he do that?"

Peanut looked back up at the ceiling. "Because I think he believes in this place. Not just leading it—but really being part of it."

Kip was quiet for a long time. Then he asked, "Do you think he knows how to end the war?"

Peanut thought of Kazik's quiet smile earlier that day, and the way he had walked away without answering their question.

"I think he knows it's not simple," she said. "And maybe... maybe it's not about one big battle or one clever plan. Maybe it's about little things. The kind of things no one puts in history books."

"Like building homes," Kip murmured.

"Or helping strangers," she added. "Or sharing food. Or being kind, even when you're scared."

Kip rolled onto his back again, staring up at her. "That's not how wars usually end."

"No," Peanut agreed. "But maybe that's why this war hasn't ended. Everyone's trying to win it... and no one's trying to end it."

They grew quiet again. The lantern dimmed to a soft orange glow, shadows stretching long across the walls. The gentle sounds of the Hollow faded into the background like a lullaby.

"I like it here," Kip whispered after a while. "I want to help. I want to be part of this."

Peanut reached over and gave his paw a gentle squeeze. "Me too."

They lay there in the quiet stillness, hearts finally calm, breaths slow and steady. For the first time in what felt like forever, they drifted toward sleep without fear.

Hope—quiet and small—settled beside them like a blanket.

And the Hollow, alive and peaceful all around them, watched over its newest souls in silence.

Chapter 8

The Choice to Stand

The days in the Hollow settled into a rhythm. Gentle, warm, and a little strange.

Morning light filtered down through cracks carved into the bark far above, turning the underground city into a soft glow of gold and orange. Sounds of life filled the air—hammering, talking, laughter, and the bubbling of water drawn from deep rivers below. Life kept moving here, even though the outside world felt like it was falling apart.

Peanut woke early most mornings, slipping out of bed to help the badger baker knead dough with strong paws and steady hands. Kip helped at the forges, carrying wood and old metal for the builders, who turned broken swords into shovels and bits of armor into plows. Pieces from the war were used for peace.

And for a while, that was enough.

But then Orin returned.

She had only been gone a few days, out with Malik and Victor, helping a new group of survivors reach safety—mothers with little ones, an antelope with an injured leg, and a fox family from the far western edge. Their return was quiet, like most things in the Hollow. No horns, no cheering. Just tired hands helping other tired hands. Sad eyes slowly lifting with hope.

Peanut and Kip ran to meet her. Orin smiled when she saw them, her eyes worn but kind.

"You're both still in one piece," she said, brushing dust off her shoulders and setting down her pack. "And no trouble reports. That's already better than Victor usually manages."

Kip grinned. "We've been helping. Every day!"

"Good," Orin said, ruffling his head. "There's more to keeping peace than knowing what's broken. It's knowing how to fix it."

Peanut paused, then asked, "Are you leaving again soon?"

Orin nodded. "Probably. A scout came through last night. Another village was attacked near the eastern ridge. We don't know if it was Varrin or Varnak this time. Doesn't matter much. The people still lose either way."

Kip's brow creased. "Can we come with you?"

Orin raised an eyebrow. "Come?"

Peanut stepped forward beside her brother. "We want to help. Really help. Not just sweep floors or carry things. We want to join the Peacebound."

Orin's smile faded a little. She looked at them closely—not angry, but like someone noticing a small flame and wondering how long it would last. "You're both brave," she said, folding her arms. "But are you sure?"

Peanut nodded. "We don't want to hide from the war anymore."

Kip nodded too. "We've seen what it does. To people. To towns. If there's a way to stop it—really stop it—we want to try."

Orin knelt in front of them. "A lot of folks think the Peacebound are heroes. That we sneak into enemy camps, rescue families, and bring down kings."

"Isn't that what you do?" Kip asked.

"Sometimes," Orin said. "But most days? We dig graves. We carry water. We sit beside people who are scared and try to help them feel strong again. We go into places that have been torn apart, and we listen. We help. And the hardest part..." Her voice got quieter. "We can't save everyone. You'll fail. You'll feel like giving up. But you'll keep going anyway."

The kids didn't speak right away.

Then Peanut said, "That still sounds like something worth doing."

Orin smiled. "You're tougher than you look."

"I'm a squirrel," Peanut said with a small smirk. "We sleep in twigs during storms."

Kip added, "And fall out of a lot of them."

They laughed—real, soft laughter.

Orin stood. "Alright then. If you're serious, we'll start small. Training. Lessons. Little jobs. You'll follow us around and see what we really do. And if, after all that, you still want to be Peacebound—we'll talk again."

Peanut and Kip looked at each other and grinned.

"We're ready," Peanut said.

"More than ready," Kip added.

Just then, Malik's heavy steps came from a nearby tunnel. The old elephant raised an eyebrow. "You recruiting kids again, Orin?"

"Looks like it," she said with a half-smile.

Victor walked in behind him, holding a basket of bandages. “As long as they don’t faint like those raccoons did, I’m all for it.”

“They’ve got grit,” Orin said. “We’ll see if they’ve got staying power.”

Malik gave a slow nod. “We’ll teach them what we can.”

And so it began.

The next morning, Peanut and Kip stood with the other Peacebound trainees in the Hollow’s old training yard—a wide cave lit by sunlight from above and the soft glow of torchlight. Wooden practice dummies stood in rows. Straw-lined circles marked places for sparring. Targets were carved into the stone for throwing practice.

It wasn’t a battlefield.

But maybe, someday, it would help stop one.

Peanut’s heart beat like a war drum.

She stood at the edge of the Hollow’s main gate, her small pack strapped tight to her shoulders, a worn bandana tied around her head to keep her ears back. Beside her, Kip adjusted his belt for the fifth time, checking that the little carving knife he had brought was still tucked into the side loop.

Today was the day.

Their first mission as Peacebound.

Victor had handed them a rough map and said, “Keep your paws light and your minds sharp.” Then he gave them a small smirk and added, “And don’t forget to breathe. The last thing I need is to carry a passed-out squirrel through the woods.”

The Peacebound had gathered quietly at dawn—Orin, Malik, and Victor among them. No big sendoff. Just a nod from Kazik as they passed through the tunnels, the old fox watching with calm eyes and a slight smile.

They left the Hollow behind and stepped into the shadowed world above.

The journey was long, the trail winding through thick woods where the trees whispered in the wind. It was only midday when they reached their destination: a small place called Elmbridge, built along the north bend of a dry riverbed.

The smell hit them first—smoke, dirt, and something heavy in the air that felt like sadness.

As they stepped from the trees, Peanut's heart sank. The village was barely standing. Just a few huts and blackened beams. Ash still covered parts of the buildings, and some roofs sagged like tired backs. There were no guards. No flags. Just silence... and eyes peeking from doorways.

Children peeked out from behind broken walls. Mothers pulled them close. An old badger sat on a stump, sharpening a hoe like it was a weapon.

Peanut reached for Kip's paw without thinking.

She had expected ruins. Maybe even a battle.

But this—this was something else.

Orin stepped forward and called out gently, "We've come from the Hollow. We bring food and medicine."

It was like a dam broke. From behind a house, a little mouse ran forward, yelling back into the village, "They're here! It's the Peacebound!"

In a flash, animals gathered from every side—squirrels, stoats, mice, rabbits, even a bear cub with one ear. Their faces were tired, but there was hope in their eyes.

Victor and Malik went straight to work unloading the carts. Bags of flour, jars of medicine, piles of blankets. Even a few books for the children. Orin set up a small clinic near the center of town, where injured villagers slowly came forward, some limping, some holding their sides.

Peanut stood still, unsure what to do—until a tiny squirrel pup tugged at her sleeve.

"Are you from the Hollow too?" the little one asked. "Is it really safe there?"

Peanut knelt beside her. "Yeah... it is."

"Do you live there with the lions and the vultures and everything?"

She smiled. "Yeah. And they're not so scary once you meet them."

The pup giggled and ran off, yelling to his friends, "They have vultures!"

Kip walked over with his arms full of blankets. "These go to the elders' hut. Wanna come?"

For the rest of the day, Peanut and Kip worked beside the Peacebound. They helped set up water barrels, pass out food, and hold crying toddlers while parents gathered supplies. It wasn't exciting. It wasn't grand.

But it felt... right.

As the sun went down and painted the broken town in gold, the Peacebound gathered around a firepit. The villagers brought what they had—some roasted roots, a few mugs of tea, and a couple of worn instruments. One fox played a soft song while the children danced, laughing for the first time in what might have been weeks.

Peanut and Kip sat near Orin, the fire crackling between them.

"This wasn't what I expected," Kip said after a long pause. "I thought we'd be fighting someone. You know... soldiers. Bad guys."

Peanut nodded. "I thought we'd be heroes."

"You were," Orin said gently. "Just not the kind you thought you'd be."

Peanut frowned. "But all we did was carry bags. And pass out soup. That's not really... special."

Orin looked toward the fire, where the children's faces danced in the light. "When kings ride into battle, they bring noise and flags. They leave behind stories—and ruins. But when you help a place like this... when you bring food to a mother who thought her kids might starve, or hold someone's hand when they feel like giving up—that's the kind of help that stays. That's what saves people."

Kip looked down at his paws. "Why don't they write stories about that?"

Orin smiled a little. "Because it doesn't build kingdoms. It doesn't burn cities or win trophies. But the Peacebound... we're not trying to build thrones. We're trying to heal what's broken. That's the kind of story we tell."

Peanut sat quietly for a moment.

Then she said, almost in a whisper, "Maybe that's the kind of hero I want to be."

Orin leaned back with a soft smile. "Then you're in the right place."

That night, as the fire burned low and stars filled the sky over a town still healing, Peanut and Kip curled up beside one another, tired but peaceful.

.

Chapter 9

The Ashes of Driftwillow

Four months later, Peanut had just turned thirteen.

Kip was still eleven, though he always reminded her that he was "almost twelve" whenever she teased him for being younger. But age didn't matter much anymore—not when every day since joining the Peacebound had been filled with more learning and growing than they ever thought possible.

They had been on over a dozen missions now—some easy, some dangerous. They had rebuilt bridges, guarded supply wagons, and even helped stop a fight between two angry clans before it turned into something worse. And through all of it, one friend had been by their side nearly every step of the way.

Victor.

At fifteen, the golden retriever was older, taller, stronger, and faster. But he never acted like he was better than them. He joked like a brother, protected them like a guard, and listened like a friend. With Victor around, things always felt easier—even when the mission didn't.

Today was one of those easy days.

"Do you ever stop talking?" Victor asked with a laugh, balancing a crate of canned vegetables on one shoulder.

Peanut walked beside him, grinning. "Only when I'm asleep. And even then, I've been told I mutter."

"You did," Kip said from behind, dragging a bag full of water flasks. "One night you called me a 'pompous goat biscuit.' Still haven't gotten over it."

Victor snorted. "What does that even mean?"

"No one knows," Kip said seriously. "Scholars are still trying to figure it out."

They all burst out laughing, their steps light as they followed a dirt path through quiet fields and tall trees. Spring was finally beating winter—flowers were blooming, and birds flew overhead like bits of color and song.

Their goal was a town called Driftwillow, near the cliffs by the western riverbend. It used to be a busy stop for traders, but lately it had fallen silent. The Peacebound hoped to bring food, supplies, and whatever help they could.

But when they reached the top of the final hill, the laughter stopped.

The air was still. Too still.

No smoke rose from chimneys. No barking dogs. No sound of carts or children playing. Just wind.

Peanut's heart dropped.

The buildings below were nothing but burned ruins. The front gate hung broken. What wasn't burned had been smashed—wood split, windows shattered, doors torn down. A deep silence filled the place, as if the town had taken one last breath... and never breathed again.

They stood frozen for a moment.

Then Victor said quietly, "Stay behind me."

They moved slowly down the hill, weapons unslung but lowered. The smell of smoke still clung to the ground, mixed with something heavier—ashes and fear. Kip stepped over a broken sign that once read: *Welcome to Driftwillow - Walk Softly, Speak Kindly.*

Now it just read: *ow - Walk So—ly, S—e K—ly.*

Peanut swallowed hard.

They walked the empty streets like shadows, eyes scanning doorways and alleys. Nothing moved. Even the animals that usually returned to ruined places—crows, rats, bugs—were missing.

Victor stepped over a broken water trough and stopped.

Something fluttered in the breeze.

It was a flag, ripped and burned—but still clear.

A golden lion, stitched in flame.

Varrin's symbol.

Kip clenched his fists. "No."

Peanut whispered, "Maybe it wasn't him. Maybe someone else—"

But Kip stormed past her and kicked a blackened barrel, sending it tumbling. "No! I knew it! Everyone thinks he's some hero, some savior! But he's just like Varnack! He destroys and walks away like it doesn't matter!"

"Kip," Victor said softly, stepping closer.

But Kip wouldn't stop. "All this time, we thought he might be better. That one side wasn't as cruel. But look! They burned *everything*!"

He picked up a scorched doll from the mud. Its face was melted and stuck with ash. He held it tightly, shaking.

Peanut stepped closer and gently placed a paw on his back.

Then a voice came from behind them.

"We need to go."

They turned and saw Orin standing at the end of the street, her face dark with sorrow.

Victor frowned. "We haven't even checked the far—"

"There's no one left," she said quietly. "I already looked. They're gone. Either they ran... or worse."

The silence grew heavier.

Peanut looked around again—at the burned wood, the broken homes, the ghost of a place that once lived. Now it was just one more wound in a world already full of them.

Orin adjusted her pack. "We need to tell Kazik. This changes things."

Victor nodded. "We'll bring proof."

Kip still hadn't moved. His eyes were locked on the burned doll.

Peanut stepped beside him and said softly, "Come on, Kip. We'll make sure everyone knows."

He looked at her, his eyes wet but full of fire. "They won't care."

She didn't look away. "Kazik will."

He blinked, then slowly stood, brushing ash from his paws.

Together, the four of them turned and began the long walk back to the Hollow—carrying the weight of a town that no longer existed...

...and a banner that should never fly again.

The Hollow felt quieter than usual.

Peanut, Kip, Victor, and Orin moved quickly through its winding paths and shaded tunnels, past stacked crates of food and softly glowing lanterns, past resting families and newcomers still trying to find their place. The usual warmth of the underground city felt dim tonight—as if even the walls were holding their breath.

They didn't stop at their homes. They didn't change out of their dusty cloaks. They walked straight through the heart of the Hollow, all the way to the upper ring—a carved-out room that looked down on the central atrium, where Kazik lived.

The old fox was already waiting.

He knelt beside a young badger, helping her tie a bundle of sticks with string. She giggled at something he whispered. Kazik smiled, gave her bundle a small tug to check it, and sent her on her way.

Only after she turned the corner did he face the team.

His golden eyes met Orin's.

"Well?" he asked.

Orin didn't pause. "Driftwillow was gone."

Kazik's face didn't change. "Casualties?"

"No survivors," she said quietly.

Victor stepped forward and placed the burned banner at Kazik's feet. The golden lion symbol was hard to see under the black edges and ash marks, but it was still there. Varrin's mark.

Kazik looked at it for a long time. Then he raised his eyes to Peanut and Kip.

"We saw it," Kip said, his voice sharp. "It wasn't the Claw. It was him."

Peanut added, "There weren't any weapons. No battle. It was just a small town. A peaceful one."

"Not anymore," Kip said through clenched teeth.

Kazik gave a small nod and said, "I feared as much."

But Peanut stepped forward, her hands tight at her sides. "You feared it. But what were we going to do about it?"

"We can't let this keep happening!" Kip shouted. "We've been helping people for months now. Carrying supplies. Fixing things. That's good—but it's not enough!"

Kazik looked at him fully. "And what would you have me do?"

There was no anger in the fox's voice—just a calm, steady patience.

Kip blinked. He opened his mouth, then closed it again.

"I..." He glanced at Peanut, searching. "I don't know."

"Fight back," Peanut said. Her voice shook. "Something. We can't just let Varrin and Varnack destroy every town and walk away."

Kazik studied both of them. Then he turned to Victor.

Victor didn't say a word. He just looked down.

It was Orin who stepped forward next. Her voice was calm but strong.

"They're right," she said. "We've spent so long trying to heal the wounds of war. But the war isn't slowing down. The fire's spreading again. And if we only put out the sparks, we'll never stop the blaze."

Kazik looked at her. His tail flicked once behind him.

Orin went on. "These two have been with us long enough. They're not just kids anymore. They've seen what this war does. They've earned the right to know the truth. About what we're really doing."

No one spoke.

Far away, the Hollow whispered—quiet voices, the clink of dishes, the roll of carts. But in this room, all was still.

Kazik stepped forward. His paw touched the scorched edge of the banner.

"I've always believed," he said slowly, "that war won't be ended by more war. Not for good. History remembers conquerors, yes... but only for a while. Their victories fade. And the pain they leave behind often grows into the next war."

He looked back at them.

"Ending this war won't come from sharper swords. Or from burning banners. Or taking thrones."

He moved toward the far wall, where an old map was carved into the stone. Seven big circles marked the ancient kingdoms.

"It will come," Kazik said, "from bringing back what they spent their lives breaking apart."

He turned toward them.

Peanut frowned. "What do you mean?"

Kazik's eyes gleamed—not with anger, but with purpose. "I mean the world is broken. Not just burned or bruised. Broken. And before the war can end, something new has to begin."

Kip blinked. "What?"

"A restoration," Kazik said. "Of what once held the world together. The Crown of Ages."

Peanut's eyes widened. "You believe it's real?"

"More than that," Kazik said. "I believe it's waiting."

The room grew quiet.

Victor let out a breath. "You want to find the Kingstones."

Kazik nodded. "One from each kingdom. Lost. Stolen. Forgotten. But still out there. Still calling. And with them... maybe a new crown can be made. One not meant for Varnack or Varrin. But for the one it was always meant for."

"And who's that?" Kip asked.

Kazik didn't answer. He just smiled.

"I don't expect you to believe old stories," he said. "Not yet. But I do believe you're ready to hear them."

He looked at Peanut and Kip.

"You want to stop the war?" he said gently. "Then it's time you understood the plan. The long plan."

Chapter 10

Journey

The chamber beneath the Hollow was quiet, lit only by the soft glow of hanging crystals. The stone walls were ancient, carved with symbols older than the kingdoms themselves. At the center stood a table marked with the seven circles of the old world—and beside it, Kazik, leaning on his staff.

"You'll go to the library," he said, his voice calm but heavy with meaning. "The one the old kings forgot."

Orin crossed her arms. "You mean the Whispervault?"

Kazik nodded. "Hidden under the roots of Mount Dural. Older than the war. Older than the crowns. It held the lost wisdom of the First Circle."

Kip wrinkled his brow. "What are we even looking for?"

"Clues," Kazik said. "Records. Stories. If the Kingstones still exist—and I believe they do—then the Whispervault is the place to start."

Peanut blinked. "Wait. You're sending us to find the hope of the world in... a library?"

Victor laughed. "Kazik always had a way with drama."

Peanut looked at Kip. "You know what this means?"

Kip nodded and put on a serious voice. "It means our great quest is to spend the next hundred years sneezing in the dust."

Peanut made a mock-serious face. "I always knew we'd die surrounded by books."

Victor smirked. "You two are a disaster."

Kazik smiled at their jokes, his eyes shining. "Laugh if you want. But don't underestimate the power of old words. History forgets—but the Whispervault remembers."

Orin stepped closer. "And you're sure it's still there?"

"Mostly," Kazik said. "The road is dangerous. It lies far to the north, past rivers and rocky hills. Through old ruins and lands where danger waits. Varnack's scouts have grown bold, and Varrin's patrols may be worse. But the vault is hidden deep beneath the roots. Few know it exists."

He walked to the table and unrolled a cracked piece of parchment. A map, faded with age.

"The trail begins at the edge of Daggerpine Ridge," he said, pointing with one claw. "You'll pass through Fern's Watch, then take the Tethered Path. But stay off the main roads. You'll draw attention if you move like soldiers."

"We'll move like shadows," Orin said.

Kazik nodded. "That's why I'm sending you."

Kip tapped the map. "So we hike across half the kingdom to find an ancient library... and just hope it hasn't crumbled into dust?"

"It hasn't," Kazik said.

"And if it has?" Peanut asked.

"Then you'll have a story worth telling," he said simply.

They stood quietly for a moment, the weight of it sinking in.

The war. The fires. The ruins. It was easy to believe that nothing could stop it. But now, at last, there was a place to begin. A direction.

A chance.

Later that night, the Peacebound gathered in the Hollow's armory. They packed supplies—dried fruit, water skins, spare cloaks, and healing wraps. Kip grabbed a long walking stick and tried swinging it like a sword. Victor winced as it knocked over a sack of apples.

"Maybe we shouldn't bring the squirrels," he said with a grin.

"We're the heart of the team," Peanut said proudly, helping pick up the fruit. "Victor's the strength, Orin's the brains, and Kip and I are the clever, charming ones with all the best lines."

Orin adjusted her satchel. "Let's hope the Whispervault hasn't forgotten what we're after."

Victor looked toward the stone ceiling, where the lantern light flickered like stars.

"Four weeks' journey," he said softly. "Through war country."

Peanut smiled. "Guess we better start walking."

Kazik saw them off the next morning. He stood at the mouth of the Hollow, just beneath the great roots that stretched into the sky like frozen snakes. Around him, children waved goodbye, and the elder Peacebound gave out small flower charms for luck.

Kazik pressed one into Peanut's paw. "Don't chase glory," he told her. "Chase wisdom." She nodded and held it close.

To Kip, he knelt and said, "Don't mistake your size for weakness. The world often bends to those it underestimates."

Then he stood and looked over the four of them—Peanut, Kip, Orin, and Victor.

"The Whispervault remembers," he said. "Find what the world forgot."

And with that, they started down the winding root-path, through the trees and toward the mountains.

The journey to the ancient library had started with hopeful steps, but hope didn't stop blisters or storm clouds.

They left the Hollow under a gray sky, each of them carrying a pack and walking with purpose. Orin led the way, steady as ever, while Kazik's words echoed in their minds: "The truth you seek lies in the Vault of Whispers. Deep in the Gloaming Vale. Don't lose each other."

That first day, Peanut and Kip were full of questions and jokes.

"Figures an old fox would send us to a dusty library," Kip grumbled, kicking a rock off the trail.

"Yeah," Peanut added, "if I wanted to read a hundred scrolls I'd have stayed in the Hollow with the bark-chewers."

Victor, walking ahead, grinned back at them. "You'll change your tune when the scrolls are full of battle tactics and ancient secrets."

"Or cookbooks," Orin said flatly. "Kazik said the truth, not treasure."

But by day four, the laughter faded.

The rain came hard and cold. Their cloaks soaked through, and their boots squished in the mud. Only Victor's careful packing kept the food dry. Twigs scratched their faces, and even Peanut's tail drooped with water.

On the fifth day, they passed the ruins of a small outpost—just blackened beams and broken weapons. No bodies. Just claw marks on the stone. Kip crouched near a cracked helmet, the sunburst of Varrin still barely visible.

That evening, they found another sign—a torn banner bearing the black sigil of the Claw, crusted in old blood.

"We're in a ghostland," Victor said as they made camp. "No one wins in places like this. They just lose slower."

That night, they camped under a ridge of jagged rocks, hiding from the wind. Their fire burned small and quick. They ate in silence, each lost in thought.

Kip offered to take first watch.

He sat near the fire pit, now just glowing coals, with his sword across his knees. The others slept beneath a tarp Orin had rigged to catch rain. For a while, all was still.

Then Kip felt it—a tingling at the back of his neck. Not a sound, but something wrong. A pressure in the dark.

He stood up, ears twitching.

Shadows moved near the rocks.

He crept toward the edge of camp.

Shapes. Low to the ground. Silent.

Two—no, three.

Not Peacebound.

Broad shoulders. Mottled armor. One had a curved blade strapped to his back. Kip had seen blades like that before.

Claw soldiers.

His grip tightened on the sword. He glanced back at the tarp.

He could wake the others. He should.

But something burned in him—pride, anger, maybe foolishness. A voice whispered: If you're ever going to be one of them—really one of the Peacebound—this is your chance.

He slipped into the trees without a sound, moving to circle the soldiers. His heart thudded, but his hands were steady.

He crept up behind a badger wearing dark metal armor.

Kip jumped.

His sword slammed into the badger's side, knocking him off balance but not down. The soldier growled and swung back, tossing Kip to the ground.

The others turned.

Too late to run.

Kip scrambled up and lunged at the next one—a skinny ferret with a long scar across his snout. Their weapons clashed, spear against blade, until Kip's sword flew from his hands.

He ducked, rolled, and grabbed a thick branch.

The badger rose again.

Kip swung wildly, hitting the ferret in the leg. But the badger tackled him from behind, crushing the air from his lungs.

He kicked and twisted, just enough to crawl free.

He was panting. The world spun. The soldiers were closing in.

They circled him.

Kip raised the branch. No fear. No running.

But before they could strike—

A golden blur slammed into the badger, knocking him off his paws.

Victor.

Peanut crashed through the trees behind him, waving a stick and shouting, "KIP!"

Orin followed, daggers raised, eyes sharp as fire.

The Claw soldiers froze—then turned and ran.

Victor helped Kip up while Orin checked the trees. Peanut ran to her brother, eyes wide.

"You mouse-brained, mud-sniffing acorn!" she shouted, shaking him. "You could've died!"

"I was just—" Kip began.

"No. No talking. You're banned from thinking for two whole days."

Victor laughed. "He did okay, all things considered."

Peanut frowned. "You did terrible. But... also kind of brave."

Kip groaned as Victor helped him limp back to camp. "I thought I could handle it."

Victor looked at him. "Sometimes, being brave means waking your friends."
Kip sighed. "Lesson learned."
As they returned to camp, the night felt darker.
The Claw was close. Too close.
But they were together. And they were still moving forward.

Tomorrow, the trail would stretch on. The rain would fall. The Vault of Whispers waited in the north.
But tonight, they would stand guard side by side.
And Kip would not be alone.

Morning came slowly, dragging a dull gray light over the wet ground. Rain still fell in soft drops, but the worst of the storm had passed. A quiet fog hung low in the trees, curling through the branches like smoke that didn't want to leave.

The night had gone by without another attack. No second ambush. No warning shouts. No more movement in the dark. But none of them had really slept.

Every snap of a twig made their hearts pound. Every owl's call made someone grip a weapon. Kip sat with his knees pulled to his chest under his damp cloak, staring into the woods with tired eyes. Victor sat beside him, chewing on a dry biscuit and pretending it counted as breakfast.

They were up before the sun had burned away the mist. Orin moved them fast, packing up in silence and checking each other's packs and cloaks without a word.
No one talked much until they'd walked a good while down the trail.

Kip trailed behind. He shuffled his feet, ears drooping. Bruises were starting to show—dark purple on his ribs, a long scratch on his arm—but he barely noticed the pain.

Peanut kept looking back at him, but she didn't say anything. She walked faster than usual, her eyes on the road ahead. Victor slowed down until he was walking beside Kip.

"Well," he said with a grin, "that went great. You really made those Claw soldiers think twice."

Kip didn't answer.

"I mean it. That badger's probably going to quit and open a bakery. Name his first pie after you."

Kip kicked a rock off the trail. "I messed up. I could've gotten everyone hurt."

Victor shrugged. "Yeah. But you didn't. And now we know we're being followed. That's something."

"I should've woken you up."

"Yeah," Victor said. "Probably."

Kip looked at him.

"But you didn't," Victor added. "And you still fought like a squirrel three times your size. That counts."

Peanut's voice came from up ahead. "It counts as reckless, was what it counts as."

Kip winced, but she didn't turn around.

Victor glanced at her. "He's sorry, you know."

"I know he's sorry," she muttered. Then after a short pause, she added, "I'm just mad because I thought he was gone."

"I almost was," Kip said quietly.

She turned then, glaring at him. "Not funny."

"Sorry."

Peanut sighed and slowed down, letting them catch up. She bumped her shoulder gently against Kip's. "Don't do that again, okay?"

"I won't."

"And if you do, take me with you next time. I yell louder."

Victor chuckled.

Soon, the air started to change—not the weather, but the smell. The scent of pine faded. Something colder filled the air. Thinner. Sharper. The trees grew fewer, and the sky stretched wider above.

Then, through the fog, they saw it.

It rose from the ground like something ancient and alive. Its peaks were jagged, covered in snow. Sharp black rocks stuck out like armor. The trail twisted upward toward it, winding like a thread through the cliffs below.

Victor whistled. "Well, hello, Mount Dural. You're taller than I thought."

Kip stared at the clouds that touched the mountaintop. "That's it? The library's up there?"

Orin nodded. "Not all the way. But close."

Peanut smiled. "At least it's not raining up."

They all laughed—tired, sore, half-soaked—but somehow lighter than before.

Ahead, the mountain waited.

Chapter 11

The Climb

If walking through days of rain had been hard, climbing a mountain was something else entirely.

Dural didn't just rise—it loomed over them. The trail twisted back and forth up steep rocks and narrow ledges. The air got thinner with each step, and every breath felt colder. Their cloaks flapped in the wind like torn flags, and the chill sank deep into their bones.

Kip couldn't feel his feet anymore. He wasn't sure if he was still walking or just dragging them behind like heavy bags.

Victor, a few steps ahead, stopped to rest his boot on a flat rock. He puffed out his cheeks. "Remind me again why we're doing this?"

"To find the old library," Kip panted, holding his knees. "Because nothing ends a war like... a really big book."

Victor grinned. "Right. I remember now. We'll read the Claw army into giving up."

"We'll throw paper at them. Really sharp paper."

"Bookmarks in their eyes!"

They both started laughing—tired, wheezy laughter that came from climbing a mountain on almost no breakfast.

Peanut, just behind them, rolled her eyes but smiled. "You two are exhausting."

"Not as exhausting as this mountain," Kip groaned, pulling himself up another ledge. "I swear it's getting taller."

Up ahead, the trail became even thinner—a narrow path pressed against the side of a huge cliff. The drop beside them disappeared into fog. Every step had to be careful. Loose rocks slipped under their feet, and the wind pulled at their cloaks like mean fingers.

Victor was joking about naming the trail "Kip's Doom" when his voice suddenly stopped.

Kip turned just in time to see Victor lose his grip.

One slip.

One second of laughter—and the golden retriever was falling.

"Victor!"

Kip dove forward.

He hit the ground, arms out, and caught Victor's paw just in time. The weight nearly pulled him off the edge, his feet slipping on the gravel, his other hand clawing at the stone.

Victor was taller and heavier than Kip had guessed. Holding him felt like trying to lift a boulder. Kip's arms shook. His fingers started to slip.

Victor's eyes were wide. "Kip—!"

"I got you!" Kip shouted. "I got you!"

But it was too much. His hands were slipping.

Peanut dove to his side, grabbing Kip around the waist. "Hold on! I've got you!" She pulled back with all her strength.

Kip's legs slid. His arms felt like they were ripping. "I can't—!"

Then Orin arrived. She planted her feet and pulled with strong arms. Her face was tight with focus. She didn't say anything.

Still not enough.

"Malik!" Orin shouted.

The ground shook as the elephant ran over.

Without a word, Malik wrapped his trunk around Kip's middle and lifted.

Kip, Peanut, and Victor tumbled back onto the trail in a heap, gasping for air.

They lay there for a while, hearts pounding.

Victor rolled over and coughed. "Okay. Maybe... no more jokes while climbing cliffs."

"Agreed," Kip said between breaths.

Peanut sat up, frowning at them. "You idiots."

"Love you too," Victor wheezed.

Malik stood over them, arms crossed, quiet as always.

Orin stepped away from the edge and let out a long breath. "We're stopping here. Rest. Now."

They found a small ledge wide enough to sit. It wasn't perfect, but at least it blocked some of the wind. Victor rubbed his shoulder. Kip moved his fingers to check if they still worked.

Peanut didn't say anything for a while. Then she nudged Kip with her elbow. "You saved him."

"I almost didn't," Kip said.

"But you did."
Victor looked at him, a little more serious than usual. "Thanks, Kip. Really."
Kip gave him a shaky smile. "Let's not do that again."

The wind howled high above, but the Peacebound sat quietly together, catching their breath beneath the shadow of the mountain.

They reached the top of Dural just after lunchtime.

The clouds had finally moved on, revealing a wide blue sky and rows of rocky mountain peaks stretching far into the distance. From up here, the world below looked like it belonged to someone else—rivers were tiny silver lines, forests looked like fuzzy green patches, and towns were just soft smudges far away.

Kip dropped onto the rocky ground and spread out his arms. "We made it," he sighed. "Tell the world—we made it!"

Victor spun around with his arms wide. "Where's our parade? Our feast? Our throne made of pillows?"
Peanut let her pack fall beside a boulder and shaded her eyes. "So... where is it?"

Orin stood a little ahead, her eyes scanning the top of the mountain. "That," she muttered, "is a very good question."

The mountaintop was quiet, cold, and empty. There were no buildings. No towers, no doors, no gates. Just rock, sky, and wind. The land sloped gently in every direction, but nothing looked special.
"Did Kazik give you exact directions?" Peanut asked, walking up beside her.

"He said the entrance would be at the top of Dural," Orin said. "He said we'd know it when we saw it."

Victor kicked at a pile of loose gravel. "Unless we're standing right on top of it and haven't noticed."

Orin pulled out her notes—small pieces of parchment with Kazik's drawings and strange riddles. "It's here," she said. "It has to be."

They started searching. Malik walked along the edge of the summit with slow, heavy steps while Orin checked the cliffs. Kip and Victor climbed over rocks and tapped at the stone with their walking sticks.

As the sun sank lower in the sky, everyone grew more tired. The excitement they'd felt at the start turned into quiet frustration. Their feet dragged. Their backs ached. Their stomachs rumbled.

By evening, they still hadn't found anything.

"Let's spread out a little more," Orin said. "If we don't see anything before it's dark, we'll set up camp and look again tomorrow."

Kip and Victor went east, still making jokes, though their laughter was quieter now. Malik looked like a big, moving shadow in the fading light, walking the cliff edge like a silent giant.

Peanut turned west, heading toward the scraggly trees near the edge of the mountaintop. The trees were short and bent from the wind, with bare branches. She wasn't even looking for the library anymore—just something to eat. Their food had almost run out, and there wasn't enough left for a full day's hike back down.

She spotted a patch of dark berries growing under a thorny bush. Not perfect, but better than nothing. She knelt down and started picking them into a fold of her cloak, checking carefully to make sure they weren't the poisonous kind. They looked like the ones Orin had shown her before.

Then something caught her eye—a strange shadow in the rock behind the berry bush.

She pushed the bush aside and found a small hole, nearly hidden by moss and old branches. It was just big enough for someone to crawl into. The rocks around it were smoother than the rest—worn down, almost like they'd been shaped by someone.

Peanut leaned closer, peeking into the darkness. The air coming out smelled dry and old, like dust and stone and something forgotten.

She pulled the little lantern from her belt and lit it, her hands shaking a bit.

With the light in one hand, she got on her knees and crawled into the opening, brushing aside moss as she went. The stone felt cool under her fingers. The tunnel got narrower the deeper she went, and she had to duck lower.

After a few feet, the ground under her hand changed. It didn't feel like solid rock anymore—it felt... empty.

She stopped. Held the lantern close.

Then the floor disappeared.

Her arms flew out. The lantern dropped. For a moment she was weightless—then something yanked her down fast. She didn't even have time to scream. The light above vanished.

And Peanut fell.

Peanut groaned as she pushed herself up from the cold stone floor.

Her lantern lay a few feet away, still glowing—though the glass was cracked and the flame inside flickered weakly. She winced and brushed dust from her fur. Her arms and legs hurt from the fall, but nothing felt broken. She stayed crouched for a moment, blinking as she looked around.

The walls were smooth and pale, not like the rough mountain stone above. They were carved with swirls and strange symbols—faded, but still beautiful. This tunnel wasn't made by nature. Someone had built it.

She picked up the lantern and held it high. There were books here.

Not many—not like the big library she had pictured—but even a few was enough. Some were tucked into small spaces in the wall. Others were buried in dust. A broken stand leaned in the corner. A torn piece of cloth hung on the wall, too faded to show what it used to be.

Her heart skipped a beat.

This was it. The Library. The one Kazik had talked about. The one from the old stories. She had found it.

"Guys?" she called, her voice echoing off the stone. "Orin? Kip? Anyone?"

No one answered.

She turned, looking for the hole she had fallen through—but there was nothing now. Only a flat ceiling far above her head. No opening. No crack. No rope. Just solid stone.

Peanut swallowed hard. "Okay. Okay. Don't panic."

She took a deep breath to calm herself. A faint breeze came from farther down the tunnel. It was cool, and it smelled like old paper and something warm. She followed it with her eyes. A heavy stone door stood a short distance away, covered in moss. Light shone through cracks around its edges, flickering like candlelight.

Peanut looked at the door, then back at the ceiling.

"Well," she whispered to herself, holding the lantern tighter, "I guess I'm not going up."

She stepped toward the door.

Kip trudged back into camp with a sad little handful of berries cupped in his cloak.

He was soaked from head to toe, covered in pine needles, and tracking mud like he had rolled in it. Victor saw him and grinned.

"Back from your great harvest, mighty forager of the wild?" the golden retriever called, spreading his arms like a proud announcer. "Tell me—will we feast tonight?"

Kip dropped down beside him and let the berries fall into their shared bowl. "You laugh now," he said, holding them up with dramatic flair. "But behold! Enough to feed half a mouse."

Victor chuckled and picked one up. "Mmm. Starvation—with a hint of flavor."

"Better than nothing," Kip shrugged, popping one into his mouth.

Orin returned from her sweep of the eastern ridge, shaking her head as she took off her cloak. "Still nothing," she muttered. "The library must be well hidden."

Victor turned to Kip. "Hey, where's your sister?"

Kip blinked. "She went west, near the trees. Probably still searching. She said she was hungry too."

Victor tilted his head. "It's been a while though, hasn't it?"

Kip glanced toward the woods. The sun was lower now, starting to dip behind the mountain. He waved it off. "She's probably being stubborn. You know how she is—won't stop until she's sure she's the one who finds it."

But even as he said it, something twisted in his stomach.

Ten minutes passed. Then twenty.

Malik returned to camp, shaking his head slowly. "Still nothing on the west side," he said.

Kip frowned. "Wait. That's where Peanut went."

Orin stood straighter. "She hasn't come back?"

"No," Kip said. "I thought maybe she took another path—"

"She wouldn't disappear without telling someone," Victor cut in, already getting to his feet. His usual joking tone was gone. He sounded worried.

Orin's voice turned sharp. "Everyone up. Lanterns on. We're going to look for her."

Kip's heart was pounding now, faster than he wanted it to. He grabbed his lantern and pulled his cloak tighter around his shoulders.

"She's tough," Victor said as they walked. "She's probably just stuck behind a rock or something, waiting for us to come dig her out."

Kip didn't laugh. He just kept scanning the trees, calling her name under his breath, hoping—begging—that she would answer.

But the forest stayed quiet.

Chapter 12

Deep Wisdom

Kip's lantern shook in his hand, more from the cold sweat on his arm than from the night air.

They had been searching the woods for what felt like hours. The sun was long gone, leaving only silver moonlight and the soft glow of their lanterns to guide them. The trees rose like dark skeletons around them, branches creaking above, whispering sounds he couldn't understand.

"Stay close," Orin said firmly. She walked ahead with her staff across her back, eyes scanning the shadows. "One wrong step, and we'll be the ones who need saving."

Kip swallowed hard. His legs ached. His throat felt dry. But the worry in his chest was louder than his tiredness.

Peanut wouldn't just disappear like this. Not without a reason.

"She has to be out here," he muttered.

Victor, walking behind him, tried to smile. "She probably found a secret door to the library and accidentally locked us out. We'll find her sitting on a throne of books, looking all proud."

Kip wanted to laugh—but he couldn't. "She better be."

The group moved deeper into the trees near the mountain's upper slope. The ground was uneven here. Roots and sharp rocks stuck out of the dirt, just waiting to trip someone who wasn't careful.

Suddenly, Victor froze. His ears perked up. He raised a hand.

Everyone stopped.

"What was it?" Kip whispered.

Victor turned toward the trees on their right. "I heard something," he said quietly. "Moving."

Kip's heart jumped. "Peanut?"

He didn't wait.

"Peanut!" he called, running toward the sound, stumbling over branches and brush.

"Kip—!" Orin hissed, but he didn't stop.

A shape moved between the trees.

"Peanut!" he yelled again, hope rising in his chest. He ran faster, heart thumping—

Then the figure burst from the bushes with a loud snarl.

It wasn't Peanut.

A huge rat, wearing broken armor and smelling like sweat and blood, charged at him with a jagged axe held high. Its yellow eyes glowed with anger. Its teeth were bared.

Kip's eyes went wide. He tried to stop—

But the rat was too fast.

Before the axe could strike, a flash of gold slammed into Kip's side—Victor, barking a warning, knocked him down and jumped in front. The axe crashed into Victor's metal arm guard with a loud clang.

More hissing sounds filled the air.

Shapes dropped from the sky—crows and vultures in armor, screeching, their claws shining in the moonlight. More rats and bats rushed in from every side, weapons raised.

Claw soldiers.

Dozens of them.

"We're surrounded!" Orin shouted, pulling out her staff. "Get in tight!"

The Peacebound moved into a small circle—Victor dragging Kip behind him, Malik slamming his fists together with a deep growl. The big elephant stepped forward and stomped the ground so hard that small rocks rolled away.

The enemy circled them, like hungry wolves.

Kip held his lantern in one paw, his short dagger in the other. His whole body shook—but not just from fear.

They were outnumbered.

They were trapped.

Peanut stood still as her lantern's warm light glowed against endless rows of stone shelves, carved right into the mountain's walls. Dust floated in the air like golden snow, stirred only by her quiet steps.

Books. Scrolls. Tablets. Ancient objects she couldn't even name sat on stands or behind glass. Some gave off a soft glow. Others were cracked, their ink faded, but still protected in this silent place.

She walked slowly down the hallway, gently brushing her fingers along the nearest shelf. Her eyes widened when she saw the words on the spine of a thick book:

"The War of the Four Crowns – Year 114."

She pulled it down and opened it. The pages were stiff and full of careful handwriting. Notes were scribbled in the corners. There were drawings, maps, and stories about old battles and broken promises. It wasn't just history—it was real. Saved. Forgotten by most, but waiting here for someone to remember.

Her paws trembled as she set it down and reached for another—this time a scroll sealed with wax. She broke the seal gently and unrolled it.

"Chronicles of the Kingstones."

Peanut leaned closer, eyes moving quickly across the words.

But then—

A voice echoed behind her. Calm and slow.

"Are you finding what you were looking for?"

She jumped and nearly threw the scroll across the room. It slipped out of her paws and fluttered to the floor. She spun around, eyes wide.

A tortoise stood just behind her, half in shadow. He leaned on a carved wooden stick, with scrolls tucked under one arm like firewood. His shell was old and worn, covered in scars. His mossy green eyes blinked slowly.

Peanut stammered. "Wh—Who are you?"

The tortoise gave a gentle smile and nodded his head. "I am Tovan, Keeper of the Whispering Halls."

She stood up straighter. "I'm Peanut. I—uh—I fell in. Through a tunnel."

Tovan chuckled. "Yes, I heard the thud. Very dramatic."

"I'm with the Peacebound," she said quickly. "Kazik sent us. We're trying to find a way to stop the war. To stop both armies before more towns get hurt."

Tovan's smile faded. He stepped closer, tapping his staff softly on the floor with each step.

"That is a good goal," he said. "But the answers you need are not always written in books. Some truths can only be found when someone is ready to carry them."

Peanut groaned and crossed her arms. "Do all ancient librarians talk in riddles?"

He smiled again. "Only the really old ones."

She gave a small huff, but a smile tugged at her lips. Still, it faded as she looked back at the scroll. "I wish I could show this to the others. Kip would love this place. Victor too. Orin... she'd probably read the whole library."

Tovan's eyes sparkled. "You could have just used the front door, you know. Instead of falling through an old air shaft."

Peanut blinked. "Wait—there's a front door?!"

The tortoise turned and began to walk. "Of course. Would you like to use it?"

She rushed to follow him, her lantern bouncing in her hand. "Yes, please! They've got to be worried sick."

Tovan led her through the maze of halls, past rooms filled with glowing globes and scrolls that reached the ceiling. Every shelf held more wonders, and Peanut glanced at each one as they passed.

But she didn't stop.

Because knowledge was important, yes.

But right now—she just wanted to see her brother again.

Kip gritted his teeth as the battle raged around him.

Swords clanged. Wings flapped. Shadows screamed.

The Peacebound were trapped, fighting with their backs to a rocky cliff near the top of the mountain. Darkness closed in on all sides. The trees looked like skeletons in the torchlight, and sparks flew every time metal hit metal.

Kip ducked under a rat's swinging axe. He stabbed upward with his sword, knocking the rat off balance and sending him tumbling down the rocks. But another took his place right away.

Above, vultures and crows circled, diving with sharp claws. One slashed Orin's shoulder. She growled and shot it through the chest.

But every time they brought one down, two more came flying in.

"Fall back! Stay together!" Orin shouted, her voice rough from shouting.

The Peacebound moved closer together, backs against the cold wall. Even Malik, big and strong, was breathing hard now, his trunk swinging back and forth.

Kip could barely see through the smoke and beating wings—but he spotted Victor.

The golden retriever was bleeding. One leg had a deep cut, and he limped, sword in hand, swinging it in tight, careful moves. Kip ran to him without thinking.

"Get behind me!" Kip yelled.

Victor laughed through his teeth. "I'm twice your size!"

"Still faster than you," Kip snapped, swinging his sword and knocking a crow out of the air.

Two Claw soldiers—badgers with rough blades—charged toward Victor's weak side.

Kip jumped in front, blocking the first attack. Sparks flew as their weapons crashed together.

Victor dropped to one knee.

Kip fought harder, blocking strike after strike, panting for breath. He didn't even notice the cut on his arm until it started to burn. Another soldier yelled. A hawk screamed above.

Then— a deep roar.

Malik.

The giant elephant reared up and slammed his trunk into the ground. Two enemies flew through the air like leaves in a storm. His tusks were red, and his eyes burned with fire.

"You will NOT touch my brothers!" he roared, stomping forward and knocking Claw soldiers in every direction.

The circle closed again. They were holding their ground—but just barely.

"We can't keep this up!" Orin shouted.

Kip felt it too. His legs shook. His arms ached. The enemies kept coming. They were backed up to the cliff now. One last stand.

Then—CRACK.

A sound like thunder split the air.

The rock wall behind them shook. A long crack appeared, glowing with dust and breaking moss.

Everyone froze—Claw soldiers and Peacebound—watching as the stone slowly opened with a groaning sound. Cold mountain air blew through the gap.

And standing in the center—

Peanut.

Her fur was dirty and full of cobwebs. She held a torch in one paw, eyes wide as she saw them. Behind her stood six figures, stepping out of the shadows. Librarians—but not like any Kip had imagined.

An owl, tall and sharp-eyed, stepped forward with a staff like a spear.

A red panda spun her staff behind his back and crouched.

A rabbit tapped her foot, ready to move.

A cat twirled a wooden rod with a flick of her tail.

A bear, calm and huge, raised his staff like a tree trunk.

And an old badger, scrolls tied to his belt, stepped forward slowly—but with strength in every move.

These weren't just book readers. These were warriors—protectors of knowledge.

The owl slammed her staff on the stone.

"Enough."

Then all six charged.

The fight exploded—bodies flipping, weapons flying, staffs cracking against armor. The librarians moved like wind, fast and strong. Every hit landed exactly where it needed to. No magic. Just skill.

One vulture dove toward the rabbit—she jumped off Malik's shoulder and kicked him from the sky with one clean spin.

The red panda rolled under a rat's axe and jabbed his staff into the rat's side, sending him flying.

Kip could only stare.

Peanut shouted, "Kip! Inside! Now!"

The Peacebound didn't wait.

Victor limped toward the door, helping Malik. Orin covered them with her daggers. Kip backed up last, still watching the librarians hold off the Claw soldiers.

Then the stone doors began to shut—slow and heavy.

The last thing Kip saw was the owl spinning her staff in a blur, knocking down three enemies like falling stones.

Boom.

The doors sealed. Darkness filled the hall—but it was peaceful. They were inside. They were safe.

Chapter 13

Truth Beneath the Dust

The doors sealed behind them with a deep boom that echoed through the stone halls, leaving only stillness and the smell of old dust.

The Peacebound stood in silence.

Before them stretched the Library of Dural—so vast Kip thought it could be the size of a whole kingdom. Shelves rose higher than trees, filled with scrolls, books, and stone tablets. Some looked so ancient they seemed more like fossils than paper. Light filtered down in soft beams from glass windows far above. Walkways, ladders, and tiny balconies wound around the walls like vines.

Kip tilted his head back. He couldn't even see the ceiling.

"I've never..." Peanut whispered.

"I mean..." Victor started, then stopped. "Guess we'll need more bookmarks."

No one laughed.

Even Victor went quiet.

They walked slowly, their footsteps soft on the stone floor. Orin paused to study a carved plaque, running her fingers along the faded symbols. Malik shook his head and let out a soft breath, like he still couldn't believe what he was seeing.

As they passed through an archway carved with stars and trees, the red panda from before waited for them. She stood calmly, her staff resting across her shoulders.

"Follow me," she said, her voice steady and clear.

They followed behind her.

"I am called Maelin," she said as they walked. Her fluffy tail swayed behind her. "I lead the Historical Wing. And since you've come seeking truth—that's what you'll receive."

She led them up a spiral stairway to a wide balcony. There, a giant mural covered the curved wall. Though it was old and faded, the picture still stood strong: a lion standing tall before a crowd of animals—some kneeling, some bowing, and some holding spears. A united kingdom.

"That," Maelin said, "was the time of the Great King. Varrin's father. His name was King Kareth."

Peanut stepped closer. "He looked... noble."

"He was," Maelin said. "He was just, wise, and strong. Under his rule, the seven kingdoms stood together. Even the poorest towns had peace. But no kingdom is perfect. And sometimes, it only takes one voice in the dark to tear everything apart."

She turned and began pacing slowly.

"His name was Varnack. He started as a simple soldier. But he began whispering lies—telling the people that the king was hiding secrets, stealing gold, and ruling unfairly. No one could prove anything. But Varnack didn't need proof—just fear. He made the people believe they were suffering because of the king."

Victor clenched his jaw. "Was any of it true?"

Maelin shrugged. "Maybe a little. All kings make mistakes. But Varnack twisted the truth to make it dangerous."

She pointed to another part of the mural. This one showed animals raising flags, fighting soldiers, and burning towns.

"The Revolt began. More and more towns joined. Hoping to end it peacefully, King Kareth invited Varnack to speak with him. But during that meeting, Varnack stabbed the king. He killed him."

Peanut gasped.

"The rebels ran. But there was no time to mourn. Kareth's son—young Varrin—took the throne and promised to crush the rebels. He chased them across the border. Varnack vanished... but when he came back, he had built something worse."

Kip stared at the last part of the mural: a black flag marked with a blood-red claw.

"The Claw," Maelin said. "No longer just a rebellion. Now a real army. Varnack gathered angry farmers, paid fighters, outcast tribes, even criminals. He promised them revenge and treasure. And that's the war you were born into."

No one said a word.

The room went quiet, filled only with the smell of ink and stone and the weight of history.

Maelin turned to face them again. Her eyes were sharp and serious. "You came here hoping to stop this war. But you must understand—this didn't begin overnight. It was built from years of pain, lies, pride, and fear. No scroll, no sword, and no single hero can fix that."

She looked at each of them in turn.

"But maybe—just maybe—together, you can."

They stood still, hearts heavy, surrounded by stories of the past.

And for the first time, they truly began to feel just how big their mission really was.

Maelin led the Peacebound deeper into the giant maze of the library, her soft steps echoing on the cold stone floor. The air smelled of old paper, dust, and something even older—like time itself. Shelves stretched high above their heads, packed with scrolls, cracked books, and leather-covered volumes with strange symbols on the covers. The place was so big, so full of knowledge, that it made them feel small. Kip suddenly realized that even if they lived a hundred years, they could never read it all.

They walked under tall arches carved with faded markings. Glass cases stood between the shelves, showing off treasures from long ago—helmets with detailed designs, shields scratched from battles, and goblets that once held royal wine. Everything sat frozen in place, quiet as statues. Maelin stopped beside one of the cases. The light of the torches flickered in her amber eyes.

"The history of the kings," she said softly, "shaped the world you live in now. These aren't just stories—they're truths, written deep into the land itself."

She pointed to an old sword lying on red cloth. Its blade was chipped, but still looked strong.

"The kings who came before were wise and fair. Their people trusted them, and the land was at peace. Even Varrin—before he was ruled by anger—had the chance to be one of those kings."

The group leaned closer as Maelin's voice grew firmer.

"But their greatness didn't come from strength alone. They didn't rule by fear. They ruled because the people chose them. Power without trust is dangerous."

At the end of the hall stood a huge door, carved with patterns and shining with seven glowing stones.

"This," Maelin said, walking to the door, "is the door to the Crown of Ages."

She placed her paw gently on the smooth wood. "The crown was made with seven gems—one from each of the seven tribes. These weren't magic. They were symbols. Each stone showed that a nation had chosen to trust their king." She looked back at them.

"When a new king was crowned, each tribe brought their Kingstone. They placed it on the crown to show their support. If the king ever broke that trust, the tribes could take their stones back. They could choose someone new."

Peanut stared at her, heart racing.

"So... if we find the Crown of Ages," she asked, "we could bring back the old way? Let the people choose a new king—and end the war?"

Maelin gave a small smile, but shook her head.

"It's not that easy. Wearing the crown means nothing unless the people believe again. This war has hurt many. It will take time to heal. But the Crown—that's where it begins."

She pushed the heavy door open. It creaked loudly, and warm golden light poured into the hallway.

Inside was a round room, untouched by age. In the center stood a stone pedestal, carved with ancient marks. And resting on it, shining like something out of a dream, was the Crown of Ages.

The Peacebound walked into the chamber in silence. No one spoke. They all felt the weight of what they were seeing—the past, the promise, and the hope it carried.

The crown sparkled, beautiful and powerful.

But in that quiet moment, each one of them understood: this was only the beginning. The hard part was still ahead—winning back the hearts of the people, ending the fighting, and helping the land heal.

Maelin's voice broke the silence.

"Now you know why Kazik sent you. This crown isn't just a treasure. It's a reminder of what was—and what could be again. But if you wish to use it, you must be ready to do more than fight battles. You must help the people believe again. Everything depends on that."

It felt like a lifetime that they all stood staring at the Crown of Ages, its golden frame glowing softly in the warm light. Each of the seven sockets waited patiently, empty but full of meaning. The room was silent—almost sacred—as if the crown itself demanded quiet. No one dared to speak. No one even breathed too loudly.

Each of the Peacebound felt the weight of it in a different way. Kip stared with wide, shaking eyes. Victor rubbed the back of his neck and let out a long breath. Peanut leaned in slowly, as if being closer might help her understand. Even Malik bowed his head, his great trunk resting low near the floor.

They had found it.

And now they knew what they had to do.

The silence shattered.

BOOM.

A loud crash echoed from above. Dust rained gently from the ceiling.

BOOM.

Again. The stone walls trembled. A low rumble passed through the floor.

"They're breaking down the door," said Orin, her voice tight with worry.

Everyone snapped out of their awe. The quiet wonder was gone, replaced by urgency.

Maelin stepped forward, her red robes brushing the floor as she moved.

"Then we have no more time."

"But the Crown—" Peanut began.

Maelin nodded. "Yes. It must be taken. The library is no longer safe."

She turned to face them, voice calm and steady even as the crashing above grew louder. "You will carry it. Take it to your home—the Hollow. Protect it. Prepare. The path ahead is narrow, but it's the one you must walk."

"What about you?" Kip asked. "The Claw will be here any second."

Maelin gave a soft smile. "We'll greet them."

"You mean... you're going to fight?" Victor asked, stunned.

The old red panda stood taller. For a moment, she didn't look old at all. Her eyes burned with strength, like a fire that had never gone out.

"Don't mistake reading for weakness," she said. "Yes, we are librarians. But we're also guardians. And truth—when it's used the right way—can break more than lies. It can break chains."

Kip stared at her.

"You'd be surprised," she said, "how many battles I've won with nothing but a staff and a page from a book."

"But they have swords. Armor. Claws—" Peanut's voice wavered. "They'll kill you."

Maelin placed a paw gently on Peanut's shoulder.

"Wisdom teaches real power," she said. "And no sword stands a chance against that."

Behind her, the other librarians stepped forward—an owl with golden eyes, a very old rabbit, a cat with a long scar on her cheek, and a massive bear with a thick wooden staff. They all stood without fear. Each one gave a small nod.

They were ready.

"We'll buy you time," said the bear, his voice deep as thunder. "Use it well."

Malik moved to the pedestal and carefully lifted the Crown. She placed it inside a strong satchel they had prepared, then slung it over his shoulder.

"Then we go."

Maelin led them to a narrow hallway hidden at the back of the chamber. A spiral staircase twisted down into dim torchlight. From there, it would lead to the old aqueduct tunnels—forgotten paths beneath the mountain.

As the Peacebound slipped into the shadows below, Kip looked back one last time. The Crown was no longer resting on the pedestal. The war had changed. And now, wisdom stood waiting for the sword.

Another crash boomed from above.

Dust fell again.

And still, Maelin and the librarians stood their ground, eyes forward, staffs in hand.

Chapter 14

Hope from Ashes

The tunnels were colder than Kip had expected.

The stones beneath their feet were slick with moss, shining with old dampness, and the air was thick with the musty scent of age. Their footsteps echoed no matter how carefully they walked. Malik led the way, hunched beneath the curved ceiling, his large frame nearly brushing the stone above. Orin fluttered ahead from ledge to ledge, her sharp eyes always scanning. The others followed quietly, the Crown of Ages tucked safely in Malik's pack.

Water trickled through narrow channels cut into the floor, and Kip couldn't shake the heavy feeling of all that rock above them. These tunnels hadn't seen travelers in years—maybe longer—and now they were the Peacebound's only escape.

"Are you sure this leads out?" Victor whispered. His voice bounced along the walls like a pebble skipping over a pond.

Maelin had given them a map—hand-drawn, marked with odd symbols and faded notes—but it was hard to read in the dim light. Kip held it close, squinting every time they passed an old torch embedded in the stone.

"It should," Kip said. "If we follow the westward flow, it'll lead to the ravine forest. After that... we're on our own."

Victor gave a weak smile. "Ravine forest. Sounds peaceful."

No one laughed.

Peanut walked beside Kip, an arrow already notched in her bow. She hadn't spoken since they'd left the chamber. Kip knew her thoughts were with Maelin and the others. His were too.

They moved deeper.

The air grew colder. The stone walls tighter. Somewhere above them, the library still stood—maybe still fighting. That thought twisted in Kip's stomach.

Then Orin gave a short, sharp chirp.

Movement.

Malik raised a hand. Everyone froze.

Rough voices echoed ahead, their speech harsh and scratchy. Kip crouched with the others behind a bend in the tunnel. He peeked around.

Five Claw soldiers waited in a junction chamber where several tunnels met. Rats, lean and sharp-eyed, dressed in scraps of black armor and armed with blades shaped like jagged bones. One was marking the wall with a claw. Another sniffed the air, his nose twitching.

"They're tracking us," Orin whispered. "Looking for the crown."

Malik lowered his pack carefully onto the stone. His voice was low and steady. "If we run, they'll follow. We end this now."

Victor grunted. "Five of them."

"Then make it quick," Malik said.

Peanut stepped forward, her bow raised. Kip drew his sword and lifted his shield, heart racing.

They struck like a storm.

Peanut's arrow flew first—fast and silent. It hit one rat in the shoulder, knocking him sideways. Before the rest could react, Malik charged. He slammed into the biggest soldier, tusks first, and crushed him against the wall with a heavy crack.

Kip rushed in, blocking a blade with his shield. The impact jolted his whole arm. He swung wide, slicing the rat's leg and sending him staggering. Victor met another soldier head-on, blades flashing in the dark, breath coming hard.

One of the rats lunged at Peanut. She sidestepped and fired into his thigh. He collapsed with a cry, sliding across the floor. She spun and drew again—fast, calm, focused.

Kip found himself toe-to-toe with a smaller rat—quick and slippery. The rat ducked under Kip's swing and slashed low, but Kip dropped to a knee, caught the blade on his shield's edge, and kicked the rat back.

Orin swept in from above, claws flashing. She raked across the face of a soldier turning toward Malik and sent him stumbling.

The Claw fought with fury.

But the Peacebound held.

Malik, limping now, used his trunk to sweep two rats off their feet. Victor, blood running down his arm, ended one with a clean cut across the chest.

Kip struck down the last with a hard swing, sending him tumbling into the wall. Silence followed. Only the sound of panting breath and dripping water filled the space.

Peanut lowered her bow. She scanned the chamber, then turned to Kip.

"You okay?"

He nodded. "Yeah. You?"

"Fine."

Victor limped toward them, wincing. "Remind me why we didn't take the stairs?"

"Because the stairs had more rats," Kip muttered.

Malik picked up the pack, the Crown still safe inside. Blood ran down one leg, but he said nothing.

"We move," he said.

They pressed on, deeper into the winding dark. The tunnels narrowed, twisted. But now the air smelled different—cooler, fresher. The scent of trees. Of open sky.

They followed it.

The walls turned from stone to earth. Roots curled down from above. The ground felt softer. A pale light shimmered ahead—silver and clear.

And then, at last, they emerged.

The tunnel opened into the ravine forest, tall trees rising beneath a night sky scattered with stars. The scent of pine filled their lungs. Wind whispered through the branches.

Kip dropped to one knee, eyes wide, chest heaving.

They had made it.

Behind them, the mountain sealed away its ancient secrets. Before them stretched the path to the Hollow—and whatever would come next.

The journey back to the Hollow was long, but strangely calm.

After the chaos and fire of the library's siege, the deep woods felt eerily still. The Peacebound moved in quiet steps beneath the thick canopy, following hidden paths and forgotten roads. Malik led them with steady certainty, guiding the group through gullies and under moss-draped arches. With the Claw now focused on the ruins of the library, their escape had gone unnoticed.

They passed no patrols. No scouts. Only the rhythm of their own footsteps and the whisper of leaves overhead.

Peanut kept her bow strung tight and slung over one shoulder, every sense sharp. Kip walked beside her, sword at his hip, shield across his back. They spoke little. Even Victor, usually unable to go a mile without a joke, had grown unusually quiet—though now and then he muttered something just loud enough to keep the silence from swallowing them.

"You know," Victor said one night as they camped beneath the roots of a hollow tree, "I always imagined our first big mission would end with a feast or a parade. Instead, I got soaked, stabbed, and chased through a rat's maze."

"You forgot the part where you almost fell off a mountain," Kip added.

Victor groaned. "Right. That too. Turns out adventure's a lot more exhausting than the stories make it sound."

"Welcome to reality," Peanut muttered, tired but amused.

It took two full days to reach the Hollow.

The cliffs opened like ancient arms as the forest floor dipped into the hidden valley. Lanterns flickered along the winding trails, casting golden light through the trees. Watchers on the high ledges spotted them and called out, lowering rope bridges across the ravine. The gates opened without question. They were home.

Without delay, the Peacebound went straight to the council lodge. Word of their return had already spread—figures turned to watch them pass, some with hope, others with quiet curiosity, and a few with growing concern. But no one tried to stop them. They climbed the hill to the large stone-and-wood hall that stood at the Hollow's center.

Kazik was waiting.

The old fox stood beside the fire pit, wrapped in a cloak of brown and gold, leaning slightly on his gnarled staff. His eyes—sharp, amber, unblinking—watched them without surprise.

Malik stepped forward and carefully removed the bundle from his back. With quiet reverence, he unwrapped the cloth.

The Crown of Ages lay within.

Even in the low firelight, it shimmered. Its golden band was polished but worn, each of its seven sockets empty, catching the light like watchful eyes.

Kazik didn't speak.

Peanut stepped beside Malik. "We found it," she said. "Just like the records said."

Victor added, "Not without a fight. Nearly got turned into Swiss cheese in those tunnels."

Kip gave him a light elbow.

Peanut continued. "We learned the truth. The crown—it's a symbol. The seven nations gave their Kingstones to whoever they chose to rule. It wasn't power that made a king. It was the people."

"The crown only shines if the people agree to light it," Malik said quietly.

Kazik's gaze didn't move from the crown.

"We barely escaped," Kip said. "Maelin stayed behind. She and the others... they held the line."

"The Claw knows now," Malik added. "They'll come."

Still, Kazik said nothing. He stepped closer and looked down at the crown. For a long moment, he simply stared.

"So," he murmured at last, "it has begun."

"You knew," Peanut said. "Didn't you?"

The fox gave a slow nod. "I suspected. The old songs, the forgotten verses—they spoke of it. I once thought it was lost forever."

"Why didn't you tell us?" Kip asked, not angry—just confused.

Kazik looked at him, eyes soft but steady. "Because hope, when placed in a myth, can be dangerous. I feared we would chase shadows and forget the real fight. But you didn't just find a crown. You found your purpose."

Victor folded his arms. "So what now? Do we hide it? Wait around?"

Kazik looked at each of them in turn—Malik, Kip, Peanut, Victor, Orin. "Tell me," he said, "what do you believe the crown should do?"

Peanut stepped forward. "It should unite the nations. The war—this whole war—is happening because no one remembers what it means to follow someone willingly. The Claw rules with fear. Varrin rules with force. But neither has the people's hearts."

"And you think this crown can change that?" Kazik asked.

"It's not the crown," she said. "It's what it stands for. If we gather the Kingstones again, if we remind the world that kings used to be chosen—not feared—then maybe we can change something."

Kip nodded. "We're ready to try."

Victor shrugged. "Better than waiting around to get invaded."

Kazik let out a long breath. Slowly, he smiled.

"Then you are further along than I hoped. I don't need to lead you. I only need to show you the path."

He turned toward the fire, voice quiet at first.

"The crown was never about gold or gems," he said. "It was a promise. Between nations. Between the powerful and the powerless. Between those who serve—and those who lead."

Then he turned back, voice stronger now.

"You were not chosen by chance. And though the road ahead will be longer than any you've walked, you won't walk it alone."

The fire crackled.

Kazik stepped forward, one paw resting gently on the golden circlet.

"It's time," he said, "to gather the Kingstones."

The morning after their return, the Hollow stirred with a quiet buzz.

Word of the crown had spread—not through proclamations or banners, but in hushed voices, passed from ear to ear. Peacebound members walking the stone corridors were met with reverent nods and sideways glances.

Whispers followed them, not of fear—but of hope. For the first time in years, that hope moved through the Hollow like fresh wind through deep roots.

Kazik summoned them to the High Chamber, a domed cavern buried deep beneath the earth. The ceiling was etched with ancient constellations that shimmered faintly above polished stone. Lanterns dangled from twisted roots overhead, casting a warm, golden light across the long table of smooth rock.

Kazik stood at its head, his staff beside him. When the group arrived, he cleared his throat and looked at each of them in turn.

"The Crown of Ages," he began, "was no longer safe here. Now that its existence is known, it cannot stay in any one place. Not even the Hollow. It must travel with you, the Peacebound."

He unrolled a worn parchment map across the table, its corners held down by smooth iron weights. His paw moved to a symbol shaped like a broad, reaching tree—its roots and branches inked in sweeping arcs.

"Your first steps must take you beyond the Hollow," he said, voice steady. "To the east, high in the hills, lies Marrathil."

The group leaned in.

"It is a city built in layers—white stone and cedar terraces rising into the cliffs. A place of art, trade, and long-held peace. Of all the nations, they have resisted the war the longest."

Victor raised a brow. "Marrathil? Sounds fancy."

"It was," Kazik said, lips twitching faintly. "But more importantly, it is ruled by one who still believes in peace."

He looked up again, expression sharpening.

"His name is Jorm. A young stag who took leadership five winters ago after his father's passing. He's quiet, thoughtful—respected. His stance has never wavered. He condemned both Varnack and Varrin for their violence, and he refused to lend soldiers to either side. Marrathil has become a haven, welcoming thousands displaced by the war."

Peanut's ears tilted forward. "So he's on our side?"

Kazik nodded once. "He is on the side of peace. That is enough."

Silence followed. A distant rumble echoed through the deeper tunnels—stone carts moving, or traders arriving—but it only deepened the stillness in the chamber.

Victor shifted his weight. "So... no pressure. Just convince a noble from another kingdom to trust us with the fate of the world."

"Not another kingdom," Orin said quietly. "A neighbor."

Victor sighed. "Still pressure."

Kip glanced at Peanut, then turned to Kazik. "We'll go."

Peanut gave a small nod. "We're in this now."

Kazik's expression softened. "It won't be easy. The roads to Marrathil cross lands watched by the Claw—and others still loyal to the lion. But if you move with care, and keep your purpose close, you will find your way."

He walked around the table, stopping before each of them.

"Peanut," he said gently, "you speak with compassion, not command. The world needs more voices like yours."

She looked down, her face warm with color.

"Kip," Kazik continued, "you carry your sword like a shield. Don't forget why you picked it up."

He turned to Victor, to Malik, to Orin.

"Each of you brings something this mission needs. Not power. Not tactics. But courage. Restraint. Wisdom."

His eyes landed on the satchel slung across Malik's back.

"You carry more than gold and iron. You carry memories—of what we once were. And hope, for what we can be again."

He pressed a paw over his heart.

"The Hollow believes in you. And so do I."

A hush settled over the room. Lantern light flickered against the curved walls. Beneath the weight of stone and the weight of purpose, the Peacebound stood still, absorbing the charge laid upon them.

Kazik gave one final nod.

"Go now. And walk in wisdom."

They turned together and began the climb toward the surface. The tunnel curved upward in a spiral, roots twisting along the ceiling, the light growing brighter with each step.

Near the top, just before they reached the final stair, Victor leaned over and whispered toward Peanut.

"So," he said, a faint grin tugging at his mouth, "we're off to change the world."

Peanut didn't answer aloud.

But in her heart, she felt it too.

No pressure.

Chapter 15

The Price of Passage

The morning air was crisp as the Peacebound stepped out from the Hollow's entrance. The scent of damp stone and moss clung to their fur as they adjusted packs and weapons. The path ahead was long—stretching to the distant city of Marrathil—but their first goal was simpler: reach the coastal town of Seabridge and find a ship to carry them across the sea.

Victor strode ahead with a wide grin, practically skipping. "Well, this was it! First stop on our epic quest to save the world. Seabridge—sounds like a place for pirates and treasure, right?"

Peanut smirked. "I'm hoping for fewer pirates and more friendly faces."

Kip tightened the straps of his shield. "Friendly or not, we need to stay sharp. No telling what waits beyond the Hollow."

Orin, quieter than most, surprised them with a sly grin as he nudged Victor. "Try not to get us arrested before we even leave the forest."

Victor raised both paws innocently. "Hey, I'm practically a diplomat."

"Diplomat of disaster," Kip muttered.

Their boots crunched softly through fallen leaves as the forest path twisted beneath old boughs. They fell into an easy rhythm, jokes flowing between steps, the tension of past battles easing under the open sky.

Victor leaned toward Peanut. "You know, you should carry a bow everywhere. You're basically a walking sniper."

Peanut rolled her eyes. "And you're basically a walking headache."

Kip chuckled. "I prefer my sword and shield. Close and personal. Unlike Victor's 'walking headache' reputation."

Orin shook her head, a rare smile tugging at her muzzle. "You all sound like an old married couple."

"Better than bored," Victor quipped.

The sun climbed higher, and the trees gave way to rolling hills dotted with wildflowers and stone outcroppings. The scent of salt hung faintly on the breeze.

"Seabridge can't be far," Peanut said, her voice calm, though anticipation flickered beneath her words.

They crested the final hill and descended into a shallow valley where the sound of waves lapping against the shore welcomed them. The town spread below—whitewashed buildings, slate roofs, and cobbled streets winding toward a bustling harbor. Ships bobbed gently on the tide, sails billowing like wings in the breeze.

Victor's excitement returned full force. "Look at that harbor! I bet there are half a dozen boats just waiting to take us wherever we want. Adventure's just a boat ride away."

Kip's expression darkened. He scanned the rooftops, then pointed. "Something's wrong."

Peanut followed his gaze—and froze.

Banners fluttered from balconies and towers: golden lions against crimson cloth.

"The Lion's emblem," Orin said quietly. "They've claimed the town."

Victor's smile faded. "Well. That's less charming."

Armored soldiers patrolled the docks, their armor shining, their swords visible. Faces peeked nervously from windows. Laughter was rare. Conversations, quiet.

Peanut's fingers brushed her bowstring. "We're walking into Lion territory."

"And I thought the Claw was bad," Victor muttered.

They moved cautiously now, sticking to alleyways and shaded paths. Every glance over a shoulder, every guard's gaze, reminded them the war they hoped to end still reached even the far corners of the world.

By the time they reached the edge of the harbor, the weight of their mission had returned in full. Seabridge was no longer just a waypoint—it was a reminder. The road ahead would not be easy. It would be filled with eyes, with danger, with power in the wrong hands.

Peanut looked to Kip, her voice low but firm. "We have to find that boat. We have to reach Marrathil. No matter what."

Victor sighed, a flicker of his usual grin returning. "So, uh... any bets on how long before we get into trouble here?"

The streets of Seabridge narrowed as the Peacebound moved closer to the docks. Lanterns swayed overhead, casting flickering gold across cobblestones slick with sea mist. The scent of salt and fish hung thick in the air. Every corner seemed to hide another soldier in golden armor, the Lion's emblem gleaming on their cloaks like a warning.

Peanut kept her hood low and her steps quick, moving beside Kip as they weaved through alleys and back lanes. The town felt wrong—too quiet, too controlled. Conversations stopped when they passed. Shutters closed. Eyes watched, but no one spoke.

When they reached the docks, the full weight of the situation came into view.

A massive fleet filled the harbor, towering ships draped in deep red and gold. Varrin's colors. His mark was everywhere—from flags on the masts to the polished breastplates of the soldiers barking orders along the piers. Crates thudded into piles. Chains clinked. Even the smaller boats further down had guards posted at their ramps, muskets slung over their shoulders.

"They're everywhere," Kip muttered. "There's no getting out of here by just asking nicely."

Peanut scanned the docks, her jaw tight. "This whole town's under Lion control. We'll be lucky to get out at all."

Victor rubbed his chin, eyes glinting as he studied the layout. "Blockade this tight, we'll need someone with... flexible morals to sneak us out."

"I don't like the sound of that," Orin said. "But he's not wrong."

The otter turned to the group, voice low. "We should split up. Smaller groups draw less attention—and we can search more ground."

Peanut hesitated. "Split up? That's risky."

Orin met her gaze calmly. "Everything's risky right now. But five of us marching together looks like a problem. Two groups might pass unnoticed."

Victor slung an arm casually around Peanut's shoulder. "C'mon, Pea. You and me—back-alley adventurers, undercover and untouchable."

She raised an eyebrow. "You've been waiting for this moment your whole life, haven't you?"

He grinned. "Absolutely."

Malik rumbled a quiet chuckle, and even Kip cracked a smile.

They agreed to the plan. Peanut and Victor would search the dockside taverns and storefronts, where secrets and sailors mingled. Kip, Orin, and Malik would circle the far end of the harbor, watching for unguarded ships—or sympathetic eyes.

Victor led the way down a crooked alley toward a listing building with sea-warped walls and peeling paint. A wooden sign hung askew above the door, painted with a red kraken wrapped around a broken anchor.

Victor stopped, beaming. "Now *this* is where you find the sort of captain we need. Smugglers. Privateers. Maybe even a pirate or two—but the kind who value coin more than questions."

Peanut stared at the door. "Pirates?"

Victor shrugged. "Technically, we're just freedom-seeking passengers."

He pushed the door open.

The inside of *The Red Kraken* was thick with noise and heat. Laughter, shouting, and sloshing mugs filled the air, along with the sharp smells of fish stew, salt, and sour wine. Every table was occupied—foxes with gold rings in their ears, gulls in ragged coats, cats and weasels leaning over whispered deals, tails twitching.

Peanut scanned the room, tense.

Victor's eyes gleamed. "See? My kind of people."

A dagger thunked into the beam beside his head.

He blinked once, slowly.

"...Mostly."

Peanut and Victor had barely taken three steps into the tavern when a group of sailors blocked their path. A scraggly raccoon with gold hoops in both ears stepped forward, arms crossed and a sneer tugging at the corners of his mouth.

"Well, well," he said loud enough for the entire tavern to hear. "Looks like the harbor's lettin' in children now."

A few chuckles rippled through the room. A wiry ferret leaned in, his grin sharp. "You two get lost? Try the bakery down the street."

Peanut's fingers twitched near her bow, but Victor raised a calming hand and stepped in front of her with a wide grin.

"Easy now, mates," he said, puffing out his chest and lowering his voice an octave. "We're just fellow sailors, lookin' for a vessel with wind in her sails and adventure in her bones."

The pirates stared.

Peanut shoved him aside. "Ignore him. We're looking for passage to Marrathil."

A beat of silence passed—then the table exploded with laughter.

"Marrathil?" the raccoon snorted. "Haven't you heard? Every ship this side of the sea's locked down tighter than a crocodile's jaw!"

Another sailor slapped the table. "Yeah, no one sails out without the Lion's blessing. Try it, and they'll burn your sails to ash and hang your ears from the mast!"

The laughter cut off with a quiet, gravelly voice from the back of the room.

"I'll take ya."

So calm. So matter-of-fact. It stole the breath from the tavern. Every head turned toward the speaker.

A grungy snapping turtle sat alone at a corner table, hunched over a bowl of stew. He didn't even glance up.

Victor's eyes narrowed. "Wait—hold on—"

But Peanut was already moving, drawn by the voice like a magnet.

Victor caught up as she reached the table. "Pea, this is a bad idea."

She didn't look back. "This was your idea. We're not getting another offer."

"Exactly," Victor hissed. "So why now? No one sane would try to sail through that blockade."

Peanut stopped in front of the turtle.

"You said you'd take us," she said.

"I did." He reached for another spoonful of stew. "Question was, how many of ya?"

"Five," Peanut replied. "Myself and four others."

The turtle gave a slow, creaking nod. "That'll cost you."

"How much?"

He named a number that made Victor choke.

Peanut didn't flinch. "We don't have that."

"Then you don't have a ride."

"We can offer half now, half when we land."

"Don't do credit," the turtle said between bites.

Peanut leaned in. "We'll work during the trip. Cleaning, lifting, tying ropes—whatever you need."

"You're a squirrel. You even know what a halyard is?"

"Nope. But I learn fast."

The turtle stared at her for a long moment. Then he chuckled—a low, gravelly sound like stones grinding together.

"Name's Captain Mossback."

"Peanut."

He turned slowly to Victor. "And you?"

"Regretting everything," Victor muttered.

The turtle stood, rising like a ship's hull breaching the sea. He was broader than he looked sitting down—built like a boulder in motion.

"Meet me by Dock Nine at midnight. No earlier, no later. You come with coin, and quiet feet."

Peanut nodded. "We'll be there."

As Mossback lumbered past them toward the door, the noise of the tavern gradually resumed.

Victor sighed. "We just signed up to sail under a pirate turtle who might sell us to the highest bidder."

Peanut smiled. "Or we just found our way to Marrathil."

Victor watched Mossback disappear through the door.

"Same thing, really."

Kip adjusted the strap of the satchel over his shoulder, glancing up at the gulls circling lazily overhead. The sea breeze carried the smell of salt and fish through the crowded streets of Seabridge, the coastal town that bustled with markets and merchants under the shadow of Lion banners.

He walked alongside Orin and Malik, weaving through the merchant stalls that lined the cobblestone streets like colorful teeth. Bright canopies flapped in the wind, and every vendor shouted louder than the last, each trying to drown out the others with sheer volume.

Malik kept his hood low and his voice lower. "Let's be quick. We don't need to draw attention."

Kip nodded. "Right. Just ask about boats. Nothing suspicious."

They stopped at a fishmonger's stall, where long silver fish hung from hooks and the tabletop dripped onto the stones. Orin leaned in casually, flicking a coin between her fingers.

"We're looking for a boat," she said. "Heading across the sea to Marra—"

Malik hissed sharply and elbowed her, but it was too late.

The fishmonger's eyes widened slightly. "Can't help you," he muttered, turning his attention to rearranging fish heads with sudden intensity.

Kip opened his mouth to try again when a voice rang out from behind.

"You three."

A Lion guard strode toward them, one paw resting on the hilt of his sword. His golden armor caught the sun, and the crimson sash across his chest marked him as a squad leader. Two more soldiers flanked him, already closing in.

Kip turned with a too-wide grin. "Hello! Can we help you?"

The guard looked them over, suspicious. "What's your business in Seabridge?"

"We're just here on vacation!" Kip said quickly, cutting off Orin before she could open her mouth. "Been planning this for weeks. You know, sun, sea, sand. Sightseeing! I've heard the clifftop views are amazing. And the statues—oh, the statues in Marrathil! They say you can see them glowing at sunrise—"

Orin groaned and elbowed him hard. "Shut. Up."

The guard's expression darkened. "You're heading to Marrathil?"

Kip froze for half a beat too long. "...For the statues."

"Come with us," the guard ordered, stepping forward. "We've got some questions."

"No thanks," Kip said, taking a cautious step back.

The guard reached for him. "Now."

Orin moved fast.

She slammed her arm into a barrel of apples stacked beside the stall. It tipped with a crash, sending apples rolling across the street like marbles.

"Run!" Orin shouted.

The guard slipped on an apple and hit the cobblestones hard, armor clanging. Kip didn't wait.

He bolted.

They tore through the marketplace, dodging carts and shoving past startled shoppers. Voices shouted behind them. "Stop them!" "Guards! Stop those three!"

More soldiers joined the pursuit. Malik led, fast and silent, weaving through a maze of alleys with practiced ease. They darted between a butcher and a bakery, flour drifting into the air as they passed. Kip coughed and brushed dust from his tunic.

"Left!" Malik called.

They veered into a narrow cut between buildings, feet pounding the ground, breath ragged. Kip clutched the satchel tight to his chest. Inside, the Crown of Ages shifted under layers of cloth and leather. They couldn't let it fall into enemy hands. Not here. Not now.

Another corner. Another alley.

And then—blocked.

Two Lion guards stood at the far end, blades drawn. Behind them, the sound of pursuing boots grew louder.

Trapped.

Orin spun, eyes scanning. "Well. That's not great."

Malik said nothing. His gaze swept the stone walls.

Kip glanced at the alley's ends, the high window ledges, the crown pressed against his ribs like a heartbeat.

No weapons. No way through. No room to run.

Chapter 16

Smoke Over Seabridge

Peanut kept her head low as they walked briskly through the sun-warmed streets of Seabridge, weaving past fruit vendors and barking sailors. Victor walked beside her, unusually quiet, his eyes sweeping the crowds. Lion banners fluttered overhead, and golden-armored guards roamed the roads with the casual menace of those who feared nothing.

"Act normal," Victor muttered from the side of his mouth.

Peanut chuckled under her breath. "You've met me, right? This is as normal as I get."

A pair of guards passed them, spears slung lazily over their shoulders. Victor tensed until they turned the corner and vanished from sight.

"I still don't trust this Mossback guy," Peanut said. "He didn't exactly come with glowing recommendations."

Victor shrugged. "He's the only one who said yes. And you're the one who leapt at the chance."

"I did not leap. I negotiated. There's a difference."

He smirked. "Sure. Let's hope his ship isn't held together with wishful thinking."

As they rounded a bend and descended the final slope toward the harbor, the sea opened before them—wide, blue, and shimmering under the afternoon light. Massive ships lined the docks, sails furled, hulls gleaming with royal crests. The Lion's fleet stood proud and immovable, blocking every passage like the teeth of a closed jaw.

And in front of it all stood a stubby, half-rotted ship that looked like it had lost a bar fight with a hurricane.

"That one's mine," Mossback said proudly, gesturing to the creaking vessel with one stubby, clawed paw. The snapping turtle captain lumbered ahead, shell cracked and dark, his mouth curled in a half-smile. "Ain't she a beauty?"

Peanut blinked. "It's... floating."

"Barely," Victor muttered.

Two Lion guards stood at the top of the boarding ramp, spears crossed, glaring down at Mossback's crew.

"Let me do the talking," Mossback grunted, not slowing.

Victor nudged Peanut and pointed toward the far end of the docks. Her stomach dropped.

Kip.

He walked in a line beside Malik and Orin, flanked by guards. They looked dirty, winded, and unarmed. The soldiers were leading them toward the largest ship in the harbor—clearly the flagship, marked by an ornate figurehead and a raised banner flapping in the breeze.

"They've been caught," Victor said, voice low and urgent.

"We've got to do something!" Peanut hissed, starting forward.

SPLASH.

Peanut spun just in time to see the first guard topple from the ramp into the sea, arms flailing. A second splash followed an instant later.

Mossback stood at the top of the gangplank, dusting his claws with a satisfied snort.

"Problem solved," he said. "Now get aboard. The tide won't wait, and neither will I."

Victor stared up at him. "Did you just—?"

"They'll dry off," Mossback said with a shrug. "Your friends better show up quick, 'cause we're takin' off—now."

Peanut paced near the edge of the dock, eyes flicking between the narrow road where the guards had led Kip, Malik, and Orin, and the warped planks of Mossback's creaking ship.

"They're not going to get far," she muttered. "Not unless we—"

"Guards! Guards!" Victor suddenly shouted, jabbing a paw behind them. "There's a thief—he went that way!"

Peanut whirled. "What are you—?!"

It only took a second for everything to fall apart.

The Lion guards escorting Kip and the others stopped mid-step, narrowing their eyes at Victor. A moment later, shouting erupted from

Mossback's ship—two soggy, furious guards had just clawed their way back onto the docks, dripping seawater and shouting about being attacked.

Their cries carried like thunder.

"Blast it," Victor hissed.

"There! They're with the turtle!" the lead guard yelled, pointing straight at them. "Stop them!"

Three guards stormed toward Victor and Peanut, fists clenched and expressions dark. The remaining two turned back toward Kip and the others, hands on their hilts.

Victor gave a sheepish grin as he backed up. "Okay... not my best idea."

"You think?!" Peanut snapped, just as a guard lunged.

She ducked the punch and drove her shoulder into his stomach, knocking him back into a pile of fishing crates. Victor twisted with another guard, the two of them stumbling and growling as they wrestled toward the water's edge.

Across the dock, Kip's fingers worked quickly on the rope binding his paws. Squirrel hands—small, nimble, and made for mischief.

Almost...

A guard stepped forward.

Kip burst into motion.

He dove low, ramming the guard's legs and toppling him backward. Orin slammed into the second soldier a heartbeat later, and Malik followed with a solid kick to the knee that dropped him with a grunt.

"RUN!" Orin shouted.

Kip scrambled to his feet, flinging the rope aside, and sprinted toward the ship, the others right behind him.

Up ahead, Victor elbowed a guard in the ribs and sent him sprawling into a stack of nets. Peanut spun and kicked another clean off the plank into the sea.

"All aboard, or I'm sailing without ya!" Mossback roared from the helm, thick arms tugging at ropes, the tiller groaning beneath his grip.

The Peacebound raced up the ramp, boots thudding.

Behind them, four guards made a final charge for the ship.

"NOW!" Peanut shouted.

Victor and Malik grabbed the gangplank and heaved. It tipped and fell with a heavy splash—taking the guards with it. One shrieked as he tumbled, followed by a cacophony of curses and flailing armor.

Cheers broke out across the deck. The sails caught the wind, and the ship began to pull away, creaking and groaning like a beast waking from slumber.

Mossback laughed, deep and gravelly. "That's how you board in style!"

But the celebration died quickly.

Peanut turned toward the bow—and her breath caught.

Five golden ships slipped from the mouth of the harbor, sails taut and blades gleaming in the sun. The Lion's fleet had spotted them—and was bearing down fast.

Peanut stepped forward, ears low, voice tight. "Captain... I really hope you've got a plan."

Mossback grinned grimly. "Aye, lass. But you ain't gonna like it."

The sea wind snapped at the sails as Mossback's ship surged forward, groaning like it might come apart with every wave. Ahead, the five golden ships of the Lion's fleet spread out across the horizon—gleaming in the morning sun like a row of hungry teeth.

Peanut gripped the rail. "Is he really—?"

"Oh no," Victor whispered. "He is."

Malik stared in disbelief. "We're sailing straight into them!"

Below deck, a loud yawn echoed up through the hatch. A brightly colored parrot poked his head above the floorboards, feathers tousled, eyes squinting against the light.

"Hey!" the parrot squawked. "Why're we moving? I was napping."

Mossback grinned. "Mornin', Polly. Want a cracker?"

The parrot scowled. "For the thousandth time—it's Paul. Not Polly. Paul."

"Sure, sure," Mossback said, already turning back to the wheel.

A second figure followed Paul up—an unusually wide, green frog with bulging eyes and an even bigger frown. He blinked. Then blinked again. Victor, trying to be friendly, stepped forward with a hand out. "Hey there. Victor."

The frog stared.

A few long seconds passed. Then, without breaking eye contact, the frog stuck out his tongue and licked one of his own eyeballs.

Victor pulled his hand back slowly. "Right... okay."

Mossback chuckled. "Don't take it personal. That's Sump. Good listener. Terrible cuddler."

Sump croaked softly and sat cross-legged on a coil of rope, gazing into the void.

"Captain," Orin called from the bow, "what's the plan here? We can't outrun five ships."

"Or go around them," Malik added, eyes scanning the flanking vessels. "They're closing in."

The Peacebound gathered at the front, watching the golden fleet draw nearer with every gust of wind. Their sails were full, their formation tight. There would be no slipping through.

"So what's the plan?" Orin asked again, voice sharp.

Mossback didn't answer right away. He was rummaging through a worn satchel beside the wheel, one claw still lazily steering. At last, he pulled out a half-full bottle, gave it a shake, and smiled at the slosh inside.

He popped the cork with his thumb.

Peanut's eyes widened. "What are you doing?"

"Quicker to go through them," Mossback said with a shrug.

And with the bottle in one hand and the wheel in the other, he turned his battered vessel straight into the heart of the Lion's blockade.

Victor's jaw dropped. "Is he serious?"

Paul fluttered up to the rigging, feathers bristling. "Oh no. He's very serious."

The ship groaned, the sea hissed, and the Peacebound braced themselves for impact—uncertain of what waited on the other side.

"Sump!" Mossback barked, one hand gripping the wheel, the other loosely holding his half-empty bottle. "Get the cannons ready!"

Sump, motionless on a coil of rope, blinked slowly. Then he gave the laziest salute imaginable—missing his own forehead by inches—before hopping below deck.

Above, Paul fluttered up into the rigging, tugging ropes and squawking into the wind. "Sails are holding! Wind's good—for now!"

Malik peered over the bow. "They're closing in. Two ahead, three on the sides. We're boxed in."

Orin turned toward the helm, gripping the rail. "What do we do? Just tell us where we're needed!"

"Go below," Mossback called. "Help Sump with the cannons. You'll know what to do when you see 'em."

Peanut, Kip, Victor, Orin, and Malik rushed below deck. The moment they entered the gun deck, they froze.

Five enormous cannons—two to each side, one to the stern—jutting from reinforced walls, patched and braced with every scrap of wood and metal imaginable. It was as if someone had stapled a fortress to a fishing boat.

Kip let out a low whistle. "These don't belong on a ship this size."

"No wonder the whole thing groans," Orin muttered.

Sump was already there, struggling to roll a cannonball half his size across the deck. He slipped and flopped onto his face with a splat.

"Here," Malik said, hoisting both the frog and the ball with one arm. Sump blinked in gratitude and bounced into motion.

The Peacebound got to work, loading and bracing the side cannons as fast as they could. When they finished, Sump croaked and waved toward the stern.

They followed—and stopped cold.

Tucked into the rear platform sat a cannon twice the size of the others. A beast of iron and rivets, aimed dead center at the fleet's heart. Next to it rested a single massive cannonball—more boulder than ammo.

Peanut stared. "How does Sump even load that?"

Victor put his hands on the ball. "We're about to find out."

Together—Peanut, Victor, and Sump—heaved and groaned, pushing it inch by inch into place. It clunked home with a deep, echoing thud.

Peanut wiped her brow. "Please tell me we never have to do that again."

They raced topside. The ship rocked under cannonfire. The two central Lion ships were now terrifyingly close, their banners snapping in the wind. Orders echoed across the water. More shots fired.

"Cannons are loaded!" Orin shouted.

Mossback didn't even turn. He stood firm at the wheel, bottle still dangling, grin curling beneath his beard. "Good," he said. "Then hold on."

BOOM.

A shot slammed into the water just off the bow, spraying the deck.

"They're firing at us!" Kip shouted.

"Just warnings," Mossback said, unfazed. "Telling us to back off."

"Well it's working!" Victor ducked as another shot screamed overhead. "I feel very warned!"

"Means we're headed the right way."

The Lion fleet loomed, their armored prows like blades against the waves.

BOOM—KRAKOOM.

Twin blasts hit the deck. Splinters flew. Orin yanked Kip behind the mast.

"Shouldn't we be shooting back?!" she yelled.

"Not yet!" Mossback called, still humming a sea shanty.

Another blast shattered the rail near the helm—obliterating the bottle in Mossback's paw. Glass flew.

He stared at his empty hand.

"That was my favorite," he said darkly.

Then, voice low as thunder: "No more warning shots."

He dropped the shards, grabbed the wheel with both paws, and spun hard to starboard.

"SUMP!"

BOOM. BOOM.

The starboard cannons roared.

The leftmost Lion ship burst in flame and splinters, its mast toppling as its deck collapsed.

Victor whooped. "Now *that's* an opening line!"

Mossback spun the wheel the other way. The Windrat tilted hard.

BOOM. BOOM.

Two more shots pounded the same vessel. The hull cracked wide, the ship listing fast. It groaned once—and sank, swallowed by smoke and sea.

"One down!" Orin shouted.

But the flagship remained.

The largest ship. Cannons bristling. Bows pointed straight at them.

Peanut's voice dropped to a whisper. "It's so close... I could throw a rock."

Mossback didn't hesitate. "Then it's time."

He spun the wheel again, bringing the stern around.

"Fire the big one!"

Below, the Peacebound braced.

KA-THOOOOOOM.

The whole ship rattled. Kip nearly fell over. A blur shot past—

Wait—"Sump?" Kip blinked.

Sump had flown across the room like a rubber ball, splatting against the far wall.

Then—*THWOK.*

He peeled himself off, bounced once, and got back to work like nothing happened.

"He's done this before," Kip muttered.

Above, the Peacebound watched the flagship.

The giant cannonball struck midship.

BOOOOOM.

The center exploded. Fire engulfed the deck. Sailors screamed, jumping for the sea. The mast cracked, the hull buckled. In moments, the ship was gone—banners slipping beneath the waves.

Silence fell.

The fleet wavered.

And then, slowly, began to retreat.

Mossback smiled into the sea breeze. Smoke curled around him like a crown.

“Now *that’s* how you thread a needle.”

And the Windrat sailed free.

Chapter 17

Into the Teeth

The Windrat sliced through the waves, creaking with every gust like a stubborn old cart rolling downhill. Behind them, the three remaining ships of the Lion's fleet lingered on the horizon—distant but determined, sails gold-bright and unyielding as wolves trailing their prey.

Peanut leaned over the side, her fur ruffling in the sharp wind. Foam and salt surged below as the ship bounced along the churning sea. "Are they still gaining?" she called up toward the wheel.

Mossback, one clawed hand on the helm and the other scratching lazily at his beard, gave a low chuckle. "If they are, they'd best start paddlin'. Windrat's got longer legs than she lets on."

Victor leaned against the railing beside her, arms crossed. "I wouldn't call that a reassuring metaphor."

But as the sun crawled across the sky, the bright blue faded to a dull steel. Then darker still—clouds rolled in like bruises, thick and heavy. The wind turned sharp, pulling at sails and fur alike. The waves stopped glistening and began to growl.

Peanut glanced upward. "That doesn't look good."

Mossback's gaze narrowed on the horizon. For the first time, his smile faded. "Blast it," he muttered. "Weather's turnin'. Should've seen it comin'."

"Should we slow down?" Kip asked, gripping the same barrel he'd clung to since breakfast.

"Slow down?" Mossback barked a laugh that had no joy in it. "Not unless you fancy bein' fish food. We're not stoppin'. We're turning."

Victor straightened. "Turning where?"

Mossback spun the wheel with a grunt. "Krakken Rock."

Victor nearly dropped the rope he was coiling. "Krakken *what*?"

"Krakken Rock," Mossback said louder. "Big ol' stone garden in the deep sea. Real pretty. Real pointy. Ships love it."

"Wait—did you say *pointy*?"

"Oh aye," Mossback said. "Sharp rocks, sudden shallows, twisting currents. A right cozy place to snap a hull in half."

Victor's eyes widened. "Are there monsters?"

"Probably. Sea beasts, whirlpools, ghosts of drowned captains... reflections that wink back at you wrong. And if you're real unlucky, you fall off the edge of the world."

Victor's face went pale. "The edge of the—what? I thought the world was round!"

"Oh sure, sure," Mossback said, nodding solemnly. "You go tell that to the last sailor who floated off the rim. If you find him, tell him he still owes me five shells and a spoon."

Victor opened his mouth, closed it, then muttered, "My gramma said the world was round... but she also named her broomstick."

As the wind began to howl louder and the rigging shuddered under strain, Peanut's eyes locked on the water ahead—and froze.

"Kip," she said softly. "Do you see that?"

He followed her gaze.

Towering from the sea were jagged spires of stone, slick with spray and black as coal. They rose like the claws of some sleeping titan, curled and waiting. Water foamed at their base, crashing with a violence that sent bursts of white mist into the air. Each stone jutted upward like a spear meant for the sky.

"That's Krakken Rock," Mossback called grimly. "Keep your paws in the boat. This part bites."

Rain began to fall, light at first, then heavier, drumming on the deck in cold rhythm. The sea lifted beneath them with each wave, heaving the Windrat higher and higher.

Peanut gripped the railing tighter, her stomach sinking.

She didn't know much about sailing. But even she could tell—

This was not a place ships were meant to go.

The Windrat sailed into death's mouth.

Black stone pillars rose around them like the spears of a forgotten giant, stabbing through the surface of the sea at cruel angles. Some leaned inward, arching like the ribs of a long-dead beast. Others twisted like tentacles, curling up from the deep as if to grasp and drag down anything foolish enough to pass through. The storm howled through the stone, its voice echoing off every jagged surface—no longer just wind, but a scream that seemed to come from the rocks themselves.

Waves towered—twenty feet, then higher—crashing and folding over themselves with violent fury. The Windrat was tossed like a leaf in floodwater. The deck rose and fell so fast it left stomachs behind. Each time the ship crested a wave, it groaned in protest, boards creaking, nails straining in their seams.

Peanut clung to the railing, slick with rain. Her fur was soaked, her heart pounding. "We're not going to make it," she whispered.

For the first time since they met him, Captain Mossback wasn't smiling. He didn't joke. He stood stiff at the wheel, jaw clenched, eyes fixed on the storm-churned sea. His knuckles were white on the wood. His tail hung low. He held his breath like even that might break the world apart.

Then came a crack like the sky splitting.

The mast—already wounded from battle—gave out. The main beam snapped in two with a deafening crack and slammed down across the deck, missing the bow by inches. The Windrat lurched sideways. Kip tumbled into Malik, who grabbed him just in time. Orin braced herself on the rigging as lightning split the sky above.

With the mast down, the ship no longer surged forward—it limped. It didn't sail anymore. It survived.

Behind them, barely visible through mist and driving rain, the shadows of the Lion's ships still followed. Their sails were full. Their pursuit was relentless.

"They're still coming!" Orin shouted over the storm. "They're gaining!"

Mossback didn't answer. His eyes stayed forward, locked on the rocks ahead. Spires of stone—sharp, close, waiting.

Then he did something no sane captain would've done.

He turned the wheel hard.

"Wait—what are you doing?" Victor shouted.

"Buying us a miracle," Mossback growled.

The Windrat dove between two jagged pillars. The stone scraped against the hull with a grating shriek, flaking wood from her sides. The ship didn't slow.

"Drop anchor!" Mossback shouted.

Malik and Orin rushed to the chain. Together, they hauled it overboard. The chain screamed as it spun. Then—THOOM—it caught.

The ship jerked like it had been punched in the gut. The crew was thrown to the deck. Peanut tasted blood where she bit her tongue. Kip landed beside her, winded and wide-eyed.

The Windrat tilted hard.

Then—mercifully—righted.

They lay still, the world roaring around them. But here, wedged between stone, they were invisible. Hidden.

They held their breath.

And one by one, the Lion's ships sailed past.

The first tore through the storm without slowing—then struck a reef. Wood split. A mast snapped like a twig. It vanished beneath the waves.

The second caught a rising wave wrong and slammed into a pillar. Its bow cracked. The sea took it in seconds.

The third tried to turn—but too late. Its hull scraped along a jagged hook of rock and tore open like paper. Water poured in. Down it went.

No one spoke.

Then Kip, voice barely a whisper, said, "That... was the scariest hiding spot in the world."

Mossback exhaled—long, slow, shaky. "Aye," he said. "But sometimes the best place to hide is where no one else is stupid enough to look."

The sea, once monstrous and loud, now rested like a sleeping beast.

Sunlight spilled over the jagged teeth of Krakken Rock, turning their obsidian edges to silver. What had looked like claws and tentacles in the storm now rose like ancient monuments—still dangerous, but quiet, still, and strangely beautiful.

The Windrat floated between them like a ghost that had survived the night.

Salt clung to everything—sails, ropes, skin, fur. The crew moved slowly, tired but alive. Sump and Orin patched the worst of the damage, lashing broken railings, hammering bent boards into place, rigging a makeshift mainmast from whatever scrap they could find. The Windrat looked worse than ever—more bundle than boat—but somehow, she still held together.

And she sailed.

With the wind behind her and the sea smooth as glass, the Windrat began a slow, steady drift toward Marrathil.

Peanut stood near the bow, the sun warm on her fur, the breeze gentle. For the first time in what felt like weeks, she wasn't bracing against wind or flame or panic. She smiled.

Behind her, a terrible sound broke the peace.

"Hrrhhhaaaaughh—BLEUURRGH."

She turned to see Victor leaning over the side of the ship, ears pinned back, one paw gripping the railing, the other clutching his stomach.

Peanut walked up beside him, Kip a step behind. "You okay there, hero?" she teased.

Kip crossed his arms. "Storm tossing the ship like a toy? No problem. Calm water and sunshine? Blerrrgghh."

Victor wiped his mouth on the back of his paw, looking pale. "Y-you know... during the storm I had something important keeping everything down. Fear. Fear of becoming fish food. Great nausea suppressant."

He opened his mouth to say more, then doubled over with another "BLAGHH."

Even Malik passed by chuckling. "Careful not to lean too far, pup. We're short on crew as it is, and I'm not diving in after your stomach."

Victor groaned something that might've been a laugh. Or another barf.

The next few days passed in a quiet rhythm.

The sea remained calm. The wind stayed steady. The Windrat limped but never faltered. Meals were shared. Repairs were made. At night, the stars blanketed the sky so thickly it seemed like the heavens themselves were watching.

The Peacebound laughed, rested, breathed again.

But as the days slipped by and the silhouette of Marrathil crept into view on the horizon, something shifted.

The laughter quieted. The smiles faded.

Because Marrathil meant the next step. The next risk. The next trial. The next war.

They had survived the sea. Survived fire, storm, and the jaws of Krakken Rock. But the land ahead held a different kind of danger.

Peanut watched the coastline sharpen, green hills rising above stone walls. Her stomach tightened. She gripped the railing beside Victor, who was now asleep in a pile of rope, his head resting in a bucket.

She didn't say anything. No one did.

But they all felt it. The weight of what they carried.

The task still ahead.

And the quiet truth that the storm was not over yet.

Chapter 18

Unwelcoming Walls

The Windrat rocked gently in the morning tide as it pulled up to one of Marrathil's creaking old docks. A horn blew from the watchtower, and gulls scattered from the rooftops in the early light.

Peanut stood near the bow with Kip and Malik, watching as the great port city came into view. The sprawling coast of Marrathil was a tangle of rooftops, sails, and rising towers. The scent of salt and spices drifted on the breeze, mingling with fresh bread and frying meat. Even from the ship, they could hear the chaotic voices of merchants already haggling with morning customers.

Peanut took a final pouch of coin from her bag and walked it up to Mossback, who stood at the wheel, guiding the ship into place. His shell was still scratched from the storm, and the cracked stump where the mast used to be had been haphazardly patched with rope and sailcloth.

"Here," Peanut said, handing him the coin. "The final payment. For everything."

Mossback turned his yellowed eyes to her paw, then grunted. "You were good passengers. Mostly. Better than some of the barnacle-brained mercs I've ferried across worse waters."

He gave her a slow, toothy grin. "Can't say I'll miss you, but I might remember you next time I need someone to patch holes and get shot at."

Peanut smiled faintly. "Thanks, Mossback."

Polly stuck his feathered head down from the crow's nest. "So that's it, then? No parade? No medals? I risked my wings for this lot!"

Mossback cackled. "Oh hush, Polly."

"For the thousandth time—Paul," the parrot muttered, hopping down to the deck.

Peanut turned to the others. Victor was helping lower the last of their bags, though he kept glancing back at the ship with a wistful look. "Not every day you get to outrun a fleet and a sea storm with a crew of lunatics," he said.

Sump waddled over, his skin still slightly green from his cannon mishap. He gave Kip an enthusiastic wave and made a bizarre motion that might have been a salute or a stretch—or both.

"I'll miss the little guy," Kip said.

Sump responded by blowing a loud raspberry and licking his own eyeball.
Victor recoiled. "Okay. I'll miss him a little less now."
Even Malik cracked a smile.

Mossback stomped over to the gangplank and gave it a good kick. "Alright, Peacebound. Get going. You've got kingdoms to fix and crowns to chase."

Peanut hesitated for a moment. "Where will you go now?"

Mossback looked out at the sea. "Wherever the wind takes us. Might head south. Or west. I've got debts to dodge and legends to chase."

"And drinks to spill," Paul added.

"Aye," Mossback grinned. "And bottles to break."

They gave one last round of goodbyes, then stepped onto the worn planks of the Marrathil docks. As they turned to go, Mossback gave a low whistle behind them.

"Don't die," he called.

"No promises," Kip said, throwing a wave over his shoulder.

From Peanut's point of view, Marrathil opened up like a flood. The streets beyond the dock were alive with sound and movement. Children darted between stalls, shouting out names of fruits and pastries. Vendors sang and shouted in competition, trying to outdo each other in volume and charm.

Roasting meat, baked bread, perfume, fish, oil, and hundreds of other scents mingled in the air until it was dizzying. The buildings leaned forward like they were eavesdropping, and colors danced on every surface—fabrics, flags, and signs flapping wildly in the morning breeze.

Marrathil was a city that breathed. The streets rippled with life, flowing like rivers around merchant stalls and street performers. Vendors called out in a dozen accents, voices sharp and fast, hawking everything from skewered shrimp to handmade jewelry to maps scrawled with dubious treasure routes. One fox in a bright red vest was juggling knives while shouting the price of his candied chestnuts. A monkey with earrings clung to a pole and pointed tourists toward his owner's stall.

The smell of food was everywhere. Roasted meat, saffron rice, citrus glaze, and something doughy and sweet rolled out of nearby bakeries. Fish sizzled on open grills beside clams soaking in garlic butter, and giant skewers turned slowly over open coals. It was enough to make Victor groan, holding his still-sensitive stomach.

Peanut noted how clean the city felt, compared to the dirt-packed roads and ruined villages they'd passed through. The streets were swept. The buildings were bright. And the guards—uniformed in green and silver—stood with an ease and familiarity that told her they were locals, not stationed soldiers from the Claw or Lion. For the first time in weeks, there were no banners of war, no sounds of marching boots, no shadow of a tyrant's eye watching the roads.

A merchant spotted Kip in the crowd and darted toward him, waving a small carved squirrel in one paw. "For you, young sir! See how the tail moves? Only three silver—"

"I'm not a child," Kip said with a smug tilt of his head, marching on like a king who'd just dismissed a court jester.

The vendor blinked, then shrugged and chased after another target.

From the higher streets, the view opened to the horizon, and there it was—rising above the city like the crown on a noble brow.

The castle.

A towering structure of white stone and golden spires. Built into the edge of a cliff, it overlooked the ocean, half fortress and half palace. Flags of deep green and polished antlers flew proudly from its towers, the symbol of House Bramble.

"Is that it?" Kip whispered.

Victor nodded. "That's King Bramble's castle, alright."

The Peacebound paused. After weeks of running, hiding, fighting, and surviving storms and armies alike, their goal was finally in sight.

“What did you mean we can’t see the king!?” Kip shouted, glaring up at the guards who blocked the castle gate with crossed spears and crossed arms. The guards didn’t even flinch. Their expressions were carved in stone.

“We’ve traveled across oceans,” Kip continued, puffing himself up. “We’ve escaped armies and storms and worse. We’re not going to be turned away by a few guards!”

Orin stepped forward, her sleek brown fur still damp from the morning’s sea mist. The otter's voice was calmer than Kip’s, but no less firm. “We’re here on official business, and we only need a short audience. It’s a matter of great importance to the king.”

One of the guards grunted, clearly unimpressed. “You and every other self-important bunch that shows up here,” he muttered.

Orin held her ground. “At least send a message to someone in the court. Perhaps Kazik—”

The mention of the war hero seemed to do little to sway them. Another guard, taller and equally grim, took a step forward. “You’re not getting in. Turn around before we decide you’re a problem.”

Kip clenched his fists, and Orin’s paw gently landed on his shoulder. Her calm voice was steady. “We’ll go.”

“But—” Kip began.

“We’ll go,” she repeated, with a glance back at the others.

Frustrated but not defeated, the Peacebound made their way back down the marble steps and into the buzzing city streets.

“Now what?” Victor grumbled as they weaved their way through the crowd.

“Lunch,” Orin said flatly. “We’ll regroup, and then we’ll come up with a real plan.”

They found a shaded eatery tucked along one of Marrathil’s broader lanes. A patio of stone and ivy wound around wrought iron tables, with the smell of sizzling fish and sweet, fried pastries wafting from the open kitchen. A glass canopy above filtered the sunlight just enough to make everything glow golden. The waitress, a sprightly lemur with too much eyeliner, handed out menus with a practiced smile.

Kip had a flaky fish pie filled with something spicy and sweet. Peanut ordered a bowl of creamy soup so thick her spoon stood upright in it. Victor, despite being seasick only a day earlier, devoured something that looked like it had been deep-fried three times. Malik delicately nibbled on root salad, while Orin sipped a dark broth and stayed quiet, clearly already lost in thought.

As the group settled into the meal, Victor suddenly snorted and pointed out the window.

"Look! Is that a jester walking the streets?" he said between bites of whatever fried delight he was consuming.

Outside, a painted figure danced down the cobblestone street, bells jingling from his hat and shoes as he spun and threw confetti at passing children.

Victor turned to the waitress. "Is it normal for clowns to be loose in the streets, or should we be worried?"

She chuckled, barely looking up as she set down more drinks. "It's for the jousting tournament. Happens every few months now. King Bramble loves them. It's become a regular event."

The group exchanged looks over half-eaten plates and shared silence that said more than words could.

A crowd. An event. A reason for the king to be present.

Orin leaned forward, her voice low. "Then that's where we'll go next."

The jousting tournament was larger and livelier than anyone had expected.

The royal field outside Marrathil's walls was crowded with colorful tents and banners snapping in the breeze—reds, greens, silvers, and golds shimmering under the sun. Music echoed through the air, mingled with the clang of armor and cheers from the excited crowd. Merchants jostled through the throng, shouting out offers of candied fruits, steaming skewers, and fried roots. Jugglers, soldiers, and children wielding wooden swords weaved between people, making the whole scene a swirling chaos.

The Peacebound moved cautiously through the crowd, listening for any information that might help them reach the king. After a series of dead ends, an older hare polishing his helmet finally provided a crucial piece of information.

"Want to see the king?" he chuckled, spitting to the side. "Only one way that happens, and that's by winning the tournament. The champion got a private audience—a fancy ceremony, speeches about honor and bravery."

Kip's eyes brightened. "Then we'll join the tournament—and we'll win."

Victor nearly choked on his drink. "You'll what?"

"We'll win," Kip repeated confidently.

Victor shook his head in disbelief. "You've never jousted before."

"Neither have you," Kip said, defensive.

Victor smirked. "True, but I know enough to say it's not easy. Especially for a twig like you."

Kip bristled. "I'm wiry."

Orin interrupted their banter with a calm voice. "He might be onto something."

Victor blinked. "You're serious?"

Orin nodded. "Proper channels won't get us near the king. If winning this tournament offers a direct path, then it's worth trying."

Malik looked doubtful. "None of us even know how to joust."

"That just makes it more interesting," Kip smiled.

Victor added with a competitive grin, "I'm not going to let him have all the glory. If anyone's charming the king, it'll be me."

Peanut rolled her eyes but said nothing.

Later, the group stood at the edge of the tournament grounds, staring at the enormous beetles they were expected to ride. Each beetle was as large as a cart, with shiny black shells and legs that clicked and skittered erratically. The beasts were wild and restless, their mandibles snapping and their riders struggling to hold the reins. Even veterans had difficulty keeping their mounts steady.

One beetle suddenly charged sideways and sent its rider tumbling into a hay bale with a heavy crash.

Kip and Victor exchanged nervous glances, swallowing hard.

"Still think this won't be hard?" Malik asked dryly.

Victor shrugged. "It looked like a dance."

"A dance with a wild beast," Kip muttered.

They approached the sign-up booth. Kip stepped forward first, heart pounding, followed closely by Victor, who wore a confident smile that barely hid his nervousness. The clerk didn't hesitate, simply writing their names down and handing each a blunt wooden lance.

"That's it?" Kip asked, eyeing the heavy pole.

"Good luck," the clerk said with a grin. "Try not to die."

Kip struggled to move under the weight of the heavy plate armor that covered him from head to toe. The metal was old and battered, and clearly made for someone much larger than he was. The breastplate pressed tightly against his chest, the gauntlets felt like clumsy iron blocks on his hands, and the greaves dug into his shins with every step. But the worst was the helmet—oversized and sealed tightly, it left him practically blind. Through the narrow eye slits, the world appeared as little more than a blur of shadows and flickering shapes.

His lance, a massive wooden shaft nearly twice his height, felt like it weighed as much as he did. The shield strapped awkwardly to his beetle's side was too large to fit properly, and they had to lash it tight with leather cords to keep it from slipping off as the beetle moved. The creature beneath him fidgeted nervously, its antennae twitching and legs stamping anxiously on the ground.

Peanut's voice cut through the noise, sharp with worry. "Kip, you don't have to do this. This armor's way too heavy, and you can barely see. It's a bad idea."

Kip swallowed hard, the weight of the helmet pressing on his jaw. "I know, Peanut," he said, though his voice was firm. "But if we want to get close to the king, this is the only way. The jousting champion gets to see him. We have to win."

Nearby, Victor struggled into his own set of armor. His pieces clanked loudly as he moved, a grimace on his face betraying his confidence. Kip couldn't help but smirk. "Looks like you're just as doomed as me."

Victor shot him a look, but before he could respond, his beetle jerked sharply to the side, its many legs scrambling on the dirt. Victor wobbled and nearly fell off. Kip's smirk widened. "Hey, looks like someone's got the jitters."

But just as Kip leaned forward to tease him more, his own beetle reared up suddenly. The huge insect's antennae lashed out, and Kip felt himself lose balance. Before he could steady himself, he was airborne, tumbling head over heels before hitting the ground with a grunt.

Peanut gasped and rushed to his side. "Are you hurt?"

Kip groaned but tried to laugh it off. "Just the armor... and the landing." He pulled himself up, brushing dust from his metal gauntlets. "No time to waste."

Orin and Malik stood close by, watching with unease. The plan to enter the jousting tournament suddenly seemed far less certain. None of them had any experience with this strange, clanking sport—and the day had only just begun.

A sharp, commanding blast from a horn echoed across the grounds. The crowd hushed and then roared in anticipation.

"The tournament has begun!" a herald's voice announced loudly.

Jousters scrambled to their mounts, gripping their lances tightly and adjusting armor plates. The giant beetles stamped and reared, their tough shells gleaming under the sun despite the storm the day before.

Kip tightened his grip on his lance, forcing himself to focus. His vision was limited, but he could make out the blur of Victor across the field. There was no going back now—not after all they'd endured.

Peanut's hand found his shoulder. "Be careful."

The crowd grew quiet as a herald stepped forward and blew a sharp whistle to get everyone's attention. He cleared his throat and called out the rules of the tournament in a loud, clear voice.

"To win a joust, a rider must knock their opponent off their beetle. If both riders stay on, the one who breaks their lance or loses control will lose the match. Since we have many riders today, there will be four rounds. If you fall off your beetle, you're out."

Kip's heart pounded in his chest. Four rounds. Four chances to prove himself—and to get close to the king.

He looked down at the beetle under him. Its legs twitched, and its antennae waved in the air. Victor's beetle wasn't any better—both bugs seemed wild and hard to control, shifting and swaying like they wanted to toss their riders off.

Then Kip noticed something different nearby. A tall greyhound sat still and proud on top of his beetle. His armor was shiny and smooth, and his bug didn't move at all. It stood with its six legs firmly planted, as calm as a statue.

Kip leaned toward a group of people standing nearby. "Who's that?" he asked.

They shared a quick laugh before one of them answered. "That's Sir Alric. He's the king's best friend—and the champion of these tournaments. He wins almost every time. You can tell—he rides like the beetle is part of him."

Kip's stomach tightened. Sir Alric looked strong and ready, like nothing around him could shake him. It was clear he was the one to beat.

"Most of the riders today are new," the man added. "Sir Alric's the favorite to win. No one stands much of a chance against him—unless they get very lucky."

Kip swallowed hard but stood up straighter. Luck or not, he had to try.

A nearby helper called out, "Kip! You're third in the first round!"

Victor gave Kip a pat on the shoulder and grinned, his eyes full of playful challenge. "Good luck out there. Try not to fall off in the first five seconds."

Kip nodded. Even though he was nervous, something steady burned in his chest. He was ready to try. As Victor walked off to get in place, Kip grabbed his lance and took a deep breath, getting ready to face his first match.

Chapter 19

Where Heroes Fall

Kip's heart thumped in his chest as he waited for his turn. His opponent was a young beaver, about his size, who looked just as nervous as Kip felt. They gave each other a quick nod—a silent way of wishing each other luck.

The herald blew his whistle again to start the match. Both riders climbed onto their beetles and held their lances tightly.

The beetles twitched and stomped, full of energy and ready to run.

"Ready!" the herald shouted.

Kip's beetle jumped forward so suddenly that he nearly fell off. He squeezed tight with his legs, trying to stay steady through every bump and shake. He didn't even try to aim—he just focused on holding on.

Across from him, the beaver's beetle charged too, its rider gripping his lance with all his strength.

The two beetles rushed at each other, fast and wild. The crowd's cheering grew louder. Kip tried to keep his lance steady, even though his hands were shaking.

Then came the hit.

The crash shook Kip from head to toe. His whole body jolted, and for a second, he thought he was going to fall.

But he didn't.

He held on.

He barely noticed the beaver's lance snap against his shield. But he did see his opponent lose balance and tumble off the beetle with a startled yell.

The announcer's voice rang out: "And the winner, Kip of the Peacebound!"

The crowd cheered, clapping and shouting his name. But Kip just sat there, wide-eyed, breathing hard.

He had done it. He had won.

Kip barely had time to catch his breath before the next match was called. His new opponent stepped forward—a huge bear whose wide shoulders nearly filled the gate. The bear's armor fit perfectly and shone in the sun. His large paws gripped a heavy lance that looked more like a tree trunk compared to Kip's.

Kip's chest tightened. The bear was at least twice his size and looked like he'd done this many times before. Kip's armor still felt too big and too heavy. The helmet pushed down on his head, and he could only see through a thin slit. His lance felt clumsy, and he struggled just to hold it straight.

The crowd grew quiet as the two riders climbed onto their beetles. Kip's beetle twitched nervously under him, its legs shaking with each step. The bear's beetle stood calm and strong, its legs thudding against the ground like drums.

Kip took a deep breath and tried to push away his fear. Ready or not, it was too late to back out.

The herald raised his flag high. For a moment, everything felt still.

Then the flag dropped.

The beetles charged forward, their many legs clattering across the ground. Wind rushed past Kip's ears. He leaned forward, gripping the saddle and trying to stay upright. His lance bounced in his hands, and he didn't even try to aim—he just focused on not falling.

The bear came closer, his lance held straight and strong.

But right before they crashed, the bear's beetle gave a wild kick and jerked to the side. The sudden move knocked the bear off balance. His huge body swayed, his armor clanging loudly as he struggled to hold on.

Kip was bouncing and shaking, but he managed to grip tighter with his legs. His beetle slipped a little, but didn't fall.

With one last wobble, the bear toppled off his beetle and hit the ground with a loud thud. Dust flew up around him, and the crowd gasped in surprise.

Kip blinked, unsure what had just happened. Then the announcer's voice rang out across the field:

"And the winner is... Kip!"

Cheers filled the air. Kip sat frozen for a moment, still trying to believe it.

He had won again.

His heart pounded in his chest, but for the first time, Kip felt a spark of hope.

Maybe he could do this after all.

Kip's heart pounded so hard he thought it might burst from his chest. The announcer's loud voice rang out across the tournament grounds: only two matches left until the final winner would be chosen—and the chance to stand before the king. The goal they had dreamed about since reaching Marrathil was almost within reach. But standing between Kip and that dream was a challenge more personal than any before.

He squinted through the narrow eye slits in his helmet, trying to see past the sunlight and dust. Then he saw him.

Victor.

Sitting tall on his beetle, armor shining silver, Victor's eyes met Kip's. A slow, playful grin spread across his face. "Well, well, Kip," Victor called loudly so everyone could hear. "Looks like you actually made it this far. Someone must've messed up. I'll have to look into that."

Kip gave a small smirk, but inside, his stomach twisted. "Yeah? Just wait 'til I send you flying off your fancy bug," he called back. But his words felt shaky. Victor was bigger, stronger, and way more used to stuff like this. Kip didn't feel ready. He wasn't sure he could win.

The flag bearers raised their banners. Kip and Victor gripped their lances tightly, shields in place. Kip's armor felt heavier than ever. The helmet made it hard to see and muffled the roar of the crowd. He tried to breathe slowly, to focus—then froze.

Something was wrong.

A rope from the beetle's saddle had gotten wrapped around his leg, holding his foot tight. He couldn't move it.

Panic rushed through him. His hands were full—one holding the lance, the other gripping the shield. There was no way to untangle it in time.

The crowd grew quiet. The flags dropped.

Suddenly, Kip's beetle charged forward like a shot. The rope yanked hard on his leg, nearly pulling him out of the saddle. Kip wobbled, struggling to stay upright. But the fear made him sharper. He leaned forward, gritted his teeth, and forced himself to hold steady. He lifted his lance and raised his shield just as Victor came rushing toward him.

They crashed together with a huge smack. The hit shook Kip all over, but the rope kept him from falling. His leg ached where it was pulled, but he stayed in the saddle.

Victor's beetle bucked in surprise, and Victor swayed hard.

Kip turned just in time to see Victor tumble off his mount and land with a heavy thud.

The crowd cheered loudly. The announcer's voice rang out: "Kip wins!"

Kip gasped for breath, shaking from the wild ride. Victor was already getting to his feet, brushing off his armor. He looked more embarrassed than hurt.

Kip let out a long breath. One more win. Just one more, and he would finally stand before the king.

Kip's breath came in short, shaky bursts as he faced Sir Alric across the arena. The champion's armor shone in the sunlight, each metal plate polished until it gleamed. Alric stood tall and strong, his eyes cool and serious as he looked down at his much smaller opponent.

"Good luck," Kip said, trying to sound brave as he raised his lance in a polite salute.

Alric gave a sneer. His voice carried easily over the noise of the crowd. "Luck? This whole tournament wasn't even worth putting on my armor," he said, a smirk spreading across his face. "You'll be lucky just to stay on your beetle."

Kip's heart thudded hard. He knew his last win had been lucky—the rope around his leg had kept him from falling. Could he stay on again? Doubt crept into his mind, but he shook it away. He had come too far to give up now.

Around him, everything seemed to slow. The noise of the crowd faded into the background, the bright flags and banners becoming a blur of color. Kip looked up at the royal stand, where King Bramble sat—a tall stag with golden antlers, watching the match with a calm, serious face. His green robes shimmered in the light, and servants stood quietly nearby.

Kip felt the weight of the moment press down on him. This was it.

Then he saw Peanut in the stands, shouting and waving wildly. Even from far away, Kip could see the trust in his sister's eyes.

That gave him the courage he needed.

The flag dropped.

Kip held his lance tight and leaned forward as his beetle charged ahead. Its legs moved in a fast blur, antennae twitching as it raced toward Alric.

Closer and closer they came. Kip braced for the hit, muscles tight, eyes focused on the silver armor ahead.

Then came the crash—hard and loud.

Everything spun for a moment, and Kip gasped.

But when he opened his eyes, he was still sitting upright. He hadn't fallen.

He looked toward Alric—hoping it was over.

But Alric was still on his beetle. He hadn't fallen either. He adjusted his lance with a calm, unreadable face and got ready for another try.

Kip's hands shook. Could he stay on again?

The flag dropped a second time, and both beetles rushed forward.

Kip gripped the reins and leaned low, getting ready for the hit.

But right before they met, Kip's beetle jumped high into the air, its front legs kicking up.

The sudden move threw off Alric's aim. His lance missed completely.

Caught off guard, Alric lost his balance. His big frame tumbled to the ground with a loud thud.

The crowd cheered wildly. Kip blinked in surprise. He had won.

Chapter 20

Before the Throne

Kip's legs shook as he was led forward to stand before the king. The too-big armor clanked with every step, and his helmet made it hard to see, but Kip kept his head bowed low to show respect. The grandstand above was filled with cheering people, but here, standing before the king, everything felt quiet and still.

King Bramble, a tall stag with golden antlers shining in the sunlight, looked down at Kip with a small smile. His voice was deep and friendly as it echoed across the courtyard.

"Well, well," the king said with a chuckle, "it looks like the smallest rider just knocked my good friend Sir Alric off his beetle. Tell me, Sir Alric—how did it feel to lose to a squirrel in armor two sizes too big?"

Sir Alric, brushing dirt from his arms, gave Kip a hard stare before standing up straight. "It wasn't the rider who won, Your Majesty. It was the beetle. That creature was the real champion."

The king laughed and clapped his hooves. "Oh, Alric. Always the good sport, even when you lose. But I think the crowd will remember Kip for quite a while."

Still kneeling, Kip felt his cheeks grow hot under the helmet. His armor clanked softly as he moved, the moment feeling almost too big for him.

King Bramble looked down with kind eyes. "It is tradition," he said, "that the winner of the tournament may ask for a reward. So, young knight—what do you wish for?"

Kip's thoughts raced. For just a second, he dreamed of piles of peanuts and sweets. But then his real reason came back to him, strong and clear.

"All I ask," Kip said firmly, "is that you hear my friends and me in private."

The king raised his eyebrows, surprised but curious. "That is a strange request," he said, "but I think I can do even better."

Soon after, Kip and his friends—Orin, Peanut, Victor, and Malik—were invited to eat with King Bramble inside the castle. The stone halls were wide and bright, with flags waving in the warm breeze. A quiet excitement filled the air as they followed the royal guards toward the feast.

The great dining hall glowed with candlelight, making the walls shine and the old tapestries glow like firelight. The long table was packed with roasted birds covered in honey glaze, fresh bread still warm from the oven, colorful fruit, and soft cheese from the southern hills. The smell of herbs and sweet spices filled the air.

Kip finally let out a deep breath as he pulled off the heavy armor. His arms and legs ached from wearing it for so long. The helmet sat beside him on a chair, and for the first time that day, things felt quiet again. His friends sat close by—relaxed but still alert. Winning the tournament had brought them here, but their mission wasn't over.

Sir Alric sat beside the king, his armor polished and perfect again. Standing next to him was a round-faced pug in fine robes, watching everything with sharp eyes and a small smile.

"This is Master Hobbs," Alric said softly. "The king's personal helper."

The pug gave a little bow. "I hope everything is to your liking," he said politely.

Kip noticed how careful Hobbs' voice sounded—nice, but too perfect to feel real.

Orin sat up straight and spoke with respect. "Your Majesty, thank you for your kindness. But we have important things to talk about—things more serious than the tournament."

King Bramble chuckled and brushed a crumb off his robe. "Ah, but the tournament was exciting, wasn't it? Kip surprised everyone."

He looked at Kip with a sparkle in his eye, then back to Orin. "But yes, go ahead. Though I think this may not be the best place for such talks."

Orin nodded. "Could we speak somewhere more private? Without so many ears listening?"

"Of course," said the king, standing and motioning for the table to be cleared. "Come with me."

As they stood to follow, Master Hobbs leaned close to Alric and spoke in a low voice. "With everything happening outside the castle, perhaps we should bring a few guards."

King Bramble waved a hoof. "No need. I'm sure Hobbs and Alric can handle any trouble. Besides, these Peacebound were checked at the gate. No surprises."

The group shared a few quiet looks but said nothing. They followed the king through a tall doorway into the throne room.

The room was huge and full of light, with high ceilings painted with scenes of old battles and peace treaties. White stone pillars rose all around, and red carpets made their steps soft. At the end stood the throne—a large wooden chair carved with pictures of trees, vines, and animals.

King Bramble sat down and rested his hands on the armrests. The torchlight glowed on his antlers as he looked at them all.

"Very well," the king said, folding his hands thoughtfully. "Let us hear this tale of yours."

Torchlight flickered across the tall throne room, casting long shadows on the smooth stone floor and the faces of the Peacebound. Kip stood beside Peanut, who stared wide-eyed and quiet, while Orin stepped forward. She stood tall and calm, but the sadness in her eyes showed the weight of their long journey.

"We were called the Peacebound," Orin began, her voice steady. "We don't serve any king or army. We follow only the promise of peace—true peace—by restoring what was lost."

King Bramble leaned forward in his wooden throne, his eyes sharp with interest. Orin kept going.

"We were led to the Grand Library, hidden under the roots of the old forest. There, among scrolls and books forgotten by time, we found it."

She looked to Malik. The elephant stepped forward and slowly pulled a bundle from the leather satchel on his back. Carefully, he unwrapped the thick cloth.

The Crown of Ages gleamed in the dim light. It was made of old gold and twisted branches, with seven empty sockets where jewels could be placed. Even without speaking, the crown seemed to hum quietly—like a deep memory from long ago.

Malik held it out.

King Bramble's breath caught. He stood and walked slowly down the steps of his throne. His hooves echoed on the floor as he reached out and took the crown. He turned it over in his hooves, staring at every mark and carved shape.

"I've only ever seen it in paintings," he whispered. "I never believed..."

His voice had changed. It was softer now, full of wonder. He glanced at the doors, then crossed the room to check that they were locked. When he returned, his voice lowered.

"I don't think I'm the king you're looking for."

The words made the room go quiet. Orin tilted her head. Kip blinked. Victor frowned.

"What do you mean?" Orin asked.

King Bramble sighed and walked back toward the throne, but he didn't sit.

"My name is Thorim Bramble. I'm the younger brother of King Jorm Bramble, the true king of this land. You may have heard of him."

Kip nodded. "He was the great king people talk about."

"Yes," Thorim said. "And three months ago... he was killed."

Silence filled the room like a heavy fog. Thorim's jaw tightened.

"He was loved by the people. He was wise. He didn't want war with Varrin. He believed we could guard our borders, keep our people safe, and let the other kingdoms fight if they wanted to. He believed peace was worth protecting—even if it made him unpopular."

"And then he was gone?" Orin asked.

"Assassinated," Thorim said. "In his room. No guards heard anything. No one saw the killer. It was quiet. Too quiet. That same night, the council told me to take the throne. 'To keep order,' they said. But they didn't even mourn him."

Peanut leaned closer to Kip, her small body trembling.

"You think the council did it?" Malik asked.

Thorim nodded slowly. "They've wanted war with Varnack's land for years. They think Varrin is stronger—that he'll win in the end. They want to join him. When Jorm said no, they got angry. And now, with him gone, they keep pushing me to agree."

"Then why haven't you?" Kip asked.

Thorim gave a tired smile. "I use my sadness like a shield. I say, 'Not yet,' and they leave me alone—for now. But I feel trapped. I don't know who I can trust anymore. Except Alric."

He looked down at the Crown of Ages again, still in his hooves. "I've heard stories about your mission. About the Peacebound. I didn't believe them... until now." His eyes were wet. "Now that I see it... and see you..."

He seemed ready to say more—maybe to ask for help or offer it.

But then his face changed.

His eyes went wide. His breath caught.

He stumbled.

One hoof grabbed at his side, then moved to his back. He gasped, a sharp, broken sound.

A dagger stuck out from his back—thin, silver, and shining faintly in the torchlight. Its handle was black as night.

Kip cried out. Orin rushed forward and caught the king as he fell to his knees. The Crown of Ages slipped from his hooves and rolled onto the stone floor with a soft clatter.

The king slumped forward.

His eyes dimmed.

His last breath slipped out in silence.

Chapter 21

The Broken Crown

A soft rustle—just a whisper of movement—caught Peanut's eye.

Her ears perked up. Behind the throne, in the flickering torchlight, something shifted.

A shadow.

"There!" she shouted, pointing. "Behind the throne!"

In an instant, Victor was beside her. They both took off running as the figure darted out from behind the throne, quick as a flash. It was cloaked, fast, and already climbing the wall near the giant stained-glass window above the throne.

"Go!" Victor shouted.

Peanut didn't stop to think.

With a crash of breaking glass and a blast of cold night air, the figure burst through the colorful window in a spray of red, blue, and gold. Shards sparkled as they rained down.

Peanut jumped.

Victor followed right after her.

They flew through the broken window, the wind slapping against them. Below, the rooftops of the castle stretched out like jagged teeth. The cloaked figure was already two buildings ahead, jumping easily over steep roofs and slippery tiles.

"Come on!" Peanut called, landing hard but light on her feet. Her claws scraped against the shingles as she ran.

Victor grunted as he landed beside her, then took off running. The two of them leapt from rooftop to rooftop under the silver light of the moon. Far below, a bell started to ring. Guards shouted from the streets.

But up here, there was only the wind—and the chase.

Inside the throne room, Kip knelt beside the fallen king, holding one of his hooves. Orin had a paw pressed gently to the wound, but they all knew it was too late. Malik stood nearby, stunned, holding the Crown of Ages tightly against his chest as King Thorim took his final breath.

Then came the crash.

Shouts echoed from the hallway. The pounding of boots.

The tall doors burst open and guards rushed in, weapons ready. Right behind them came Sir Alric, his eyes already scanning the room. Beside him walked Master Hobbs—the king's short, round aide—his sharp eyes locking right onto the three crouched beside the king's body.

"You!" Hobbs shouted, his voice full of fury. "What have you done?!"

Orin stood slowly, raising her paws. "Wait—please listen. The king was—"

"Silence!" Hobbs barked, stepping forward. His voice turned cold and loud. "Drop your weapons and stay where you are! You've killed the king!"

"No," Kip said, stepping in front of Orin. "Someone else did this—he was stabbed, and—"

"I said silence!" Hobbs shouted again. "You can save your lies for the dungeon!"

Alric didn't speak right away. He stared at the king's still body, his face hard to read. When his eyes turned to the Peacebound, there was something in his expression—doubt. He didn't look certain.

But still, he gave a slow, unhappy nod.

"Take them," he said. "Put them in the cells. We'll find out what really happened later."

Kip didn't fight back as the guards grabbed him and pulled his arms behind his back. Orin stayed calm while they locked chains around her wrists. Malik lowered his head as the guards took the crown from his arms, even though he had held it so tightly.

The throne room filled with the sound of boots and rattling chains.

Above them, cold moonlight shone through the broken glass window, lighting up the floor with bits of red, blue, and gold—like a promise that had shattered.

Wind whipped past Peanut's face, cold and sharp. Shingles blurred under her feet as the rooftops rushed by in fast, staggering leaps. The figure ahead—a dark blur of cloth and speed—ran across the pointed roofs like a shadow on the move.

Peanut chased without stopping.

Each jump came naturally. Where others might have slipped on the steep angles and slick tiles, she flew. Her paws landed sure and steady, her tail flicked for balance, and her muscles moved like they had been trained for this her whole life.

Behind her, Victor clattered over the roofline, struggling to keep up. "Slow down!" he called.

But she didn't.

The shadowy figure made a sharp turn and slipped a little on the slanted roof. That pause was all she needed.

Peanut pushed forward, her legs pumping faster. She closed the gap. The figure slipped again—boots scraping, arms flailing—and as it leaned near the edge, she jumped.

She slammed into the figure from behind, sending them both tumbling. They hit the rooftop hard, legs and arms tangled.

The figure gasped and rolled, twisting around fast and pulling a shining dagger from its cloak.

Peanut dodged the first strike just in time—the blade hissed past her face. She backed away, heart pounding.

Another stab. She ducked, then threw herself forward without thinking, crashing into the figure again. They both fell off the edge of the roof. They hit the cobblestone below with a heavy thud.

Peanut landed on top, breath knocked from her chest. For a second, neither of them moved.

Then she noticed—the dagger had fallen. It lay on the ground between them, just out of reach.

They both saw it. And both dove for it.

Their hands touched it at the same time.

Peanut's paw closed around it first—but just then, Victor slammed into the figure, pulling them off her.

The dagger clattered away again.

Victor pinned the figure down. "Who do you work for? Who sent you?!"

The figure squirmed and hissed like an animal.

Peanut got to her feet, still shaking. She grabbed the figure's arm—and then gasped.

The arm came off in her grip.

Victor jumped back as the tail broke loose too, twitching once on the ground. The lizard slipped free like it was made of water, fast and slippery.

But it didn't run.

Instead, it pulled out a small glass vial filled with glowing green liquid—and drank it.

"No—stop!" Victor shouted. He jumped again, slamming the lizard down.

Peanut grabbed its other arm.

Too late.

The lizard's breath slowed. Its eyes turned glassy. In moments, it stopped moving.

Dead.

Peanut stared, breathing hard. "Did it just... kill itself?"

Victor didn't answer right away. He knelt there, still watching the body. "This wasn't some street thief. Someone trained them to do this."

Shouts rang out from the street.

Doors opened. Lights came on in windows above them. The sound of guards running grew louder.

"We have to go," Victor said, jumping to his feet. "Now."

Peanut hesitated. "But—shouldn't we show them—?"

"No time," he said, grabbing her arm. "They won't believe us. Not after what happened back at the castle."

"But—"

"Peanut. Trust me."

She looked at the body one last time. A strange mark on its forehead caught her eye—an eye inside a half-moon.

Then she nodded.

Together, they disappeared into the shadows.

The cold air in the lower halls of the castle clung to Kip's fur like a wet blanket. His arms were tied behind his back, and the guards' grip stayed tight as they marched him deeper and deeper into the dungeon below the throne room. Every step of their boots echoed off the stone walls.

"We didn't kill him!" Kip said for the fifth time. "You have to listen—we were trying to help!"

"Quiet," one of the guards snapped from up ahead.

"But we were with him when it happened! He trusted us! He asked us to come!" Kip's voice cracked. "Ask Alric! Ask the pug!"

A guard behind him shoved his shoulder, making him stumble. "You'll get your chance to talk."

Malik walked beside Kip, his large paws tied too. He let out a long sigh. Orin followed behind, quiet now, but her jaw was tight and her eyes burned with focus, like she was trying to see through the stone walls themselves.

"This is a setup," Kip muttered. "It has to be. Someone wanted the king dead, and now they're blaming us—"

"From their point of view, we were the only ones in the room," Orin said at last. Her voice was low. "No one else saw what we did. No shadow. No assassin. Just us... and the king's body."

Kip frowned, thinking hard. "Wait. Peanut."

"She shouted something. Right before the crash. And then she and Victor jumped through the window. I—I don't know why. Were they just trying to run?"

He tried to remember it clearly, but everything was a blur. The king falling. The dagger. The shout. The glass shattering.

"I can't remember what she said," Kip whispered.

They reached the bottom of the stairwell. A heavy iron door creaked open, and ahead was a short hallway filled with rusted bars and the sour smell of old air. The cell they were thrown into was small—just a stone room with no windows, thick walls, and one weak torch flickering at the end of the corridor.

The guards shoved them inside and slammed the door. Keys rattled. The lock clicked. Then the guards were gone.

Kip dropped to the ground, his head in his paws.

"I don't understand," he said. "We found the Crown. We were trying to do the right thing. Why does every path just lead to another prison?"

Malik sat down cross-legged on the floor, glancing at the damp walls. "I don't know."

Orin paced once, then leaned against the bars. "Someone didn't want that king to keep talking. Whoever it was—they knew exactly when to strike."

They all went quiet.

Then Malik asked, "What do we do now?"

Kip didn't answer.

Orin kept her eyes on the door. "Wait."

"For what?" Kip asked.

Malik's voice was soft. "For Peanut. And Victor."

He looked at both of them. "They're out there. Maybe they saw something. Maybe... they can help."

Kip let his head fall back against the wall with a soft thud.

"I hope so," he whispered.

They crouched beneath a crooked overhang, swallowed in shadow. The alley around them was slick with moonlight and silence, but farther up the street, the clatter of boots and shouting voices still echoed faintly—guards calling out, doors opening, questions flying through the night.

Peanut pressed herself against the wall, ears twitching. She heard the faint scrape of metal on stone where the lizard's body had fallen, and she shivered.

"What are we going to do now?" she asked softly.

Victor didn't turn. He was watching the street from the corner, one paw resting on the hilt of his dagger, though no one had come. His shoulders were stiff, like he was trying to carry the weight of the whole night on his back.

"I don't know," he said quietly.

"We left Kip," Peanut whispered. "And Orin. And Malik. They were with the king when he died. We just jumped out a window and left them behind."

"They'll be fine," Victor said quickly. Too quickly.

"You don't know that!" Peanut snapped. Her voice came out louder than she meant. "It looked like we murdered the king. They're going to blame us!"

Victor finally turned to face her, his eyes serious.

"Then we'll have to find the real killer."

Peanut blinked. "The real killer was that lizard in the street. And he's dead."

Victor shook his head. "No. I mean the people behind him. The ones who gave him the order. The ones who wanted the king gone. The council."

Peanut stared at him. A cold thought slowly rose in her mind.

"The council?" she said. "You think they were behind this?"

"I think it's the best lead we've got," Victor said. "We know King Bramble didn't want to join Varrin's war. But the council did. Maybe they were waiting for the right moment to get rid of him. A way to make it look like someone else did it."

Peanut's heart thudded. "Right before he died," she whispered, "he told us he didn't trust his own court. That someone close might betray him. That he felt trapped."

Victor nodded. "He was right."

A long silence settled between them, broken only by far-off shouting and the rustling wind. Peanut wrapped her arms around herself.

"So... what do we do?"

Victor let out a slow breath. "We find whoever's responsible. We prove who they are. And we clear our names."

Peanut looked up at him. "How?"

Victor glanced toward the lamplight at the edge of the alley. "First, we figure out who that lizard was. Who he worked for."

Peanut nodded. "The tattoo."

Victor turned back to her. "Yeah. That eye and crescent symbol. It has to mean something. Maybe a guild. Or an assassin's group. Something hidden."

"We need to find someone who knows what it means."

They fell quiet again. But this time, it didn't feel like fear—it felt like a promise.

Victor pulled his cloak tighter around his shoulders. "Come on. We have to move before the guards search this part of the city."

Peanut followed him into the shadows, her heart pounding, her thoughts racing. They had one goal now: find the truth before it was too late.

Chapter 22

Tea and Daggers

"Where are we even going?" Peanut whispered, her eyes darting across the darkened street.

Victor offered a crooked smile. "Let's just say... my time with the Peacebound wasn't all bread and blankets."

She frowned. "What?"

He glanced back at her as they walked, his hood pulled low, voice hushed. "I did some sneaking. Listening. Delivered messages no one was supposed to read. Turns out I'm a decent spy."

Peanut didn't smile.

Victor caught her look and sighed. "Okay. Look, I'm trying to keep it light. Helps me think."

She didn't reply.

He nodded to himself and led her down a sloping back alley where crooked stone steps vanished beneath the tangled roots of a dead tree. Before they reached the door below, Victor paused and pointed at a faint symbol carved into the corner of the doorway—an eye inside a crescent moon.

"I saw this earlier when we were running," he murmured. "I learned to spot a few of these during my time with the Peacebound. It's a sign—this place deals with contracts. Hired blades. Assassins."

Peanut swallowed and followed as he knocked softly on the crooked wooden door set into the wall.

A narrow slit creaked open, spilling a line of light across the dark.

"We're closed," came a voice. Gravelly. Wary. "Come back tomorrow."

"I'm looking to hire someone," Victor said smoothly.

A pause. "Hire for what?"

Victor leaned closer. "Someone to take care of something for me. Or someone—if you get my drift."

The slit slammed shut. Peanut blinked. "Did that... work?"

They stood in silence for a moment. Then—click—one lock turned. Then another. A final bolt dragged open, and the door creaked just wide enough to let them slip through.

A mole stood behind it—small, hunched, and twitchy, eyes blinking hard against the lamplight. He glanced at Victor, then at Peanut.

"Get in. Quick."
They did.
The mole closed the door behind them and immediately held out a paw.
"Money first."

Victor looked at Peanut. She frowned, then reached into the pouch Mossback had given her. She opened it just enough to flash the glint of silver coins.

The mole nodded. "Fine. This way."

They moved through a cramped hallway, ducking beneath hanging beams and following the mole deeper underground. The air turned damp, and the sound of muffled voices echoed ahead.

Victor tried to speak. "I'm Victor, by the way."
"Mole," the mole replied without turning. "Just Mole."
"Right."

At the end of the tunnel, Mole pushed open another door. Bright light spilled into the space, stinging Peanut's eyes. Inside, two mismatched tables sat on a wide, stone floor. A group sat at one—three hunched figures laughing over drinks. Their laughter stopped the moment the newcomers walked in.

Mole led them to the empty table and gestured for them to sit. "Seems like these two caught your man."

A sleek black cat at the far table turned slowly. Her golden eyes were sharp and unreadable. She wore a deep violet cloak, one ear nicked at the top. A stack of coins clicked softly under her paw as she counted them.

"He's dead then?" she asked without looking up.
Peanut leaned forward, squinting. "How did you know—?"
Then she stopped. The tattoo. The way she spoke. The way the others watched her.

"Shame," the cat said with a sigh. "Good assassin, that one. Quiet. Quick. Loyal. Oh well."

She went back to counting, voice light, almost bored. "So."
She still didn't look up.
"Tell me why I shouldn't just kill you both now."

"Well," Victor said, brushing off his tunic and standing, "this is just unprofessional. If this is how you treat customers, I'll be taking my business elsewhere."

He barely stood before a hulking alley cat—gray, scarred, and solid muscle—stepped out from behind and shoved him back into his chair. The wood groaned under the impact.

"Wrong answer," purred the sleek black cat.

She flicked a silver coin between her claws with practiced ease, golden eyes gleaming in the lamplight. The room stayed quiet, every eye on her.

"But," she added smoothly, "because I'm in a good mood tonight... I'll let you try again."

Victor glanced sideways at Peanut, who sat frozen. Slowly, she straightened and found her voice.

"We're not here to hire a killer," she said. "We're Peacebound."

That made the cat pause.

"Peacebound?" she repeated, finally lifting her gaze to study them. "Who sent you, then?"

"Kazik," Peanut said without hesitation. "He trusted us with a mission. An important one."

The cat leaned forward slightly, eyes narrowing.

"If Kazik really sent you... then tell me." She tapped a claw on the table. "What leg did he limp with?"

Victor and Peanut froze. They glanced at each other.

Then Peanut said, "He doesn't limp. I've seen him hauling crates. Running with kids. He moved just fine."

The cat stared. Then, slowly, she smiled.

"Good," she said. "It was a trick question."

She leaned back and swept the rest of her coins into a velvet pouch. "You can call me the Baroness."

Victor blinked. "You're the Baroness?"

She ignored him and turned back to Peanut. "So, why were Peacebound sneaking around a royal castle?"

Peanut hesitated. "We're on a mission to stop the war. To bring the countries together. For peace."

The Baroness clicked her tongue and chuckled. "Well, I'm sorry you had to get tangled in all this."

She poured herself a drink, raised it in mock salute. "Nasty business, killing kings and all. But in the end... it's just business."

Peanut's fists clenched. "This isn't a game. A king was murdered. Our friends are being blamed."

The Baroness tilted her head, unbothered. "I knew Kazik long ago. Back when I was just a kitten, digging through alleys. He helped me once. This repays the debt."

Peanut didn't know whether to feel grateful or angry.

"We have friends in the castle," Victor said quietly. "Three of them. Kip, Malik, and Orin. They're being held for the murder."

The Baroness shook her head. "Can't help you there."

She stood, stretching. "But hey... if you ever need someone to..." She mimed a bulging-eyed throat-slice. "You know. Give me a call."

She waved a paw.

"Get them out."

The burly alley cat returned, grabbed them both by the arms, and shoved them back the way they came. The door slammed behind them.

They stood in the alleyway, blinking in the sudden cold and quiet.

Peanut let out a frustrated groan. "Well. That led nowhere."

Victor rubbed his shoulder and stared at the door. "Maybe not."

The dungeon stank of mildew and rusted iron. Sir Alric moved slowly between rows of barred doors, his polished boots splashing through shallow puddles that mirrored the torchlight in his hand. Shadows danced along the walls, long and jagged, as if they, too, were prisoners.

He stopped in front of the cell holding the Peacebound.

Inside, Kip sat against the wall with his arms wrapped around his knees. Orin paced like a caged wolf, silent but coiled. Malik lounged on the low bench, quietly dragging a bent nail across the stone floor to keep it sharp.

Alric stood in silence until Kip noticed him.

"Sir Alric?" Kip rose slowly, blinking. "What are you doing down here?"

Alric peered through the bars, his eyes tired. "I came to speak with you. All three of you."

Orin stepped in front of Kip, posture tense. "Come to gloat? Or checking if we've confessed yet?"

"No," Alric said, his voice low. "I came because... I don't think you did it."

The three froze.

He lowered his voice further. "King Bramble was my friend. A good friend. He trusted me more than anyone. But even then... there were things he only hinted at. He didn't trust the council—not all of them. Said some had plans of their own. Quiet loyalties."

His words hung in the damp air.

"Now he's dead. Just like his brother Jorm. And somehow, the blame lands on you."

"We didn't do it," Kip said quickly.

"I know. I believe you." Alric stepped closer, barely above a whisper now. "But if I try to free you, they'll know I suspect them. Then we lose our only chance of stopping whatever this is."

He glanced down the corridor. Still alone.

"I need to know... do you have any idea where your friends went? The squirrel and the golden retriever."

Orin narrowed her eyes. "Oh sure. You're just trying to *help* them. Not like you'd hand them over."

Malik crossed his arms. "Bit obvious, don't you think? No offense."

Alric didn't flinch. "You have every right to doubt me."

Kip stepped forward anyway. "They jumped out the window. Chased the one who really did it."

Orin shot him a sharp look, but Kip pressed on.

"They didn't have a plan. Or a destination."

Alric nodded once. "Then where would they run?"

Kip thought. He pictured Victor's hand grabbing Peanut's. The rush through shattered glass. No time to think, only escape. Then a memory surfaced—the docks. A creaking ship. A voice like gravel soaked in seawater. The weathered face of a snapping turtle with kind eyes and a slow, steady way of speaking.

"Mossback," Kip whispered. "They'd go to Mossback."

Alric frowned. "Mossback?"

"He's a pirate. Or used to be. Helped us once. If Peanut panicked, he'd be the one she'd trust."

Alric nodded slowly. "Then I'll find him. And them."

He turned to go, but Kip stepped to the bars again.

"Wait. You'll need something to prove I sent you. Something she'll believe."

Alric turned.

"Tell her..." Kip hesitated. "Tell her 'Fluffbottom said it's all gonna be okay.'"

Orin let out a bark of laughter. Even Malik chuckled.

Alric raised a brow. "Fluffbottom?"

Kip groaned. "She'll believe it."

A rare smile tugged at Alric's mouth. "Alright then. Fluffbottom."

He gave a single nod, then disappeared into the gloom, leaving only the torchlight—and a glimmer of hope—behind.

Victor pulled Peanut into a narrow alleyway between two shuttered shops, checking over his shoulder before slipping into the shadows. The street behind them pulsed with noise—distant voices, clattering hooves—but here, the silence wrapped around them like a cloak.

Peanut frowned. "What was it?"

Victor scanned the alley one last time, then reached into his vest and pulled out a folded slip of parchment. The edges were creased and frayed, the paper soft from being pressed against his chest.

"I grabbed this," he said, "off the Baroness' table. While you were distracting her."

Peanut's eyes widened. "Victor. She's the kind of cat who would've noticed if a coin blinked out of existence. You're lucky we got out alive."

"Yeah, well," he muttered, "figured if we were about to die, I might as well die being useful."

He unfolded the paper and held it out.

Peanut leaned in, squinting at the parchment. The handwriting was elegant and slanted, inked in sharp strokes like claw marks across the page.

To Whom the Task Is Given,

The king was to die. By blade, poison, or claw—it matters not. The payment will be delivered in full: twenty blood-jewels upon completion, as well as pardons for all involved, once Ironfang ascends the throne.

Keep the crown intact. No loose ends.

—Ironfang

Below the signature, a wax seal: deep red, stamped with a wolf's fang piercing through a crown.

Peanut's breath caught. "Ironfang," she whispered. "A codename?"

Victor nodded grimly. "Whoever it is, they're already powerful. Feared. And now… they want the throne."

Peanut shook her head, as if trying to clear it. "This is it. This is what we needed—proof that someone on the council planned the murder."

"But it's just the start," Victor said. "Catching the assassin isn't enough. We've got to get to the top of this, or Kip and the others are going to pay for something they didn't do."

Peanut folded her arms, thinking. "We need somewhere safe to hide. Somewhere we can figure out our next move."

Victor hesitated. "You're thinking Windrat, aren't you?"

She nodded. "It's the only place I trust in this whole city. Mossback may be a grump and a scoundrel, but he saved our lives. And he hates the council as much as we do."

Victor let out a slow breath. "Alright. But if he tries to ransom us for a barrel of saltfish, I'm blaming you."

Peanut smirked. "Deal."

The fog over the harbor curled around crates and masts like lazy ghosts. Lanterns swayed gently from the docked ships, their glow catching on salt-worn ropes and weathered planks. Peanut and Victor moved quickly, hoods up, sticking to shadows.

The Windrat loomed ahead—crooked, quiet, and familiar. Its patchwork sails were tied down, and the hull creaked with the slow pull of the tide.

Peanut let out a breath. "Let's hope Mossback's still here."

Victor raised an eyebrow. "You're sure he'll help us again?"

"He helped us once," Peanut said. "That's more than we've got anywhere else."

They stepped toward the gangplank—but a figure emerged from behind a stack of barrels, tall and cloaked, blocking their path.

Victor reacted first. "Run—!"

"Fluffbottom said it's all gonna be okay!" the figure called out, loud and clear.

Peanut froze mid-step.

Her jaw dropped. She stared.

Victor blinked. "Fluff... what?"

She grabbed his arm. "Wait. No. That's real. Only Kip would know that."

The figure stepped forward into the lantern glow—Sir Alric, cloak wrapped tight, eyes scanning the dark behind them.

"Where is he?" Peanut demanded, already striding toward him. "Where's Kip? Orin? Malik?"

"In the dungeons," Alric said. "Safe, for now. But that can change quickly. The council's tightening its grip."

Peanut's fists clenched, but Victor stepped in, voice urgent. "We found them. The ones who did it. The assassins."

Alric's eyes sharpened. "Go on."

"They operate out of a tavern near the outer wall," Peanut said. "A cat called the Baroness runs it. She knew Kazik. She knew everything."

Alric listened in silence, then shook his head. "Even if we rounded up every blade in that den, it wouldn't be enough. They're tools. Someone else is giving the orders."

He lowered his voice.

"One of my contacts—someone I trust—received an invitation. A private meeting. Tonight."

"What kind of meeting?" Victor asked.

"The kind where power changes hands behind closed doors. With both kings gone, the council's moving quickly to crown someone else. But not publicly. They want to choose in secret. Quiet. Controlled."

Peanut narrowed her eyes. "And you want us to help you crash it."

Alric nodded. "Exactly. If we can get inside—see who's really behind this—we can stop them before they make it official. Before the wrong name ends up on the throne."

"But you can't go as yourself," Victor said.

"No," Alric replied. "I need outsiders. People they wouldn't recognize. And I trust Kip's judgment."

Peanut looked toward the Windrat, then back to Alric.

"I don't trust many people anymore," she said. "But if Kip trusts you... we'll help."

Victor exhaled slowly. "This is going to get messy, isn't it?"

Chapter 23

Calm Before the Storm

The alley was narrow, damp, and smelled faintly of brine and rotting fruit. Overhead, clotheslines swayed in the early breeze, and shadows clung to the stone walls like reluctant memories of the night.

Sir Alric stood beneath a crooked overhang, cloaked and hooded. His armor was hidden beneath a long coat, but the hilt of his sword still caught the first glints of morning light.

Peanut and Victor approached cautiously, their footsteps muffled by the grime-slick cobblestones. Alric nodded once as they arrived.

"The meeting is scheduled for tomorrow night," he said without preamble. "Every high-ranking member of the royal court. They're calling it a 'strategic discussion'—but it's not. It's a takeover."

Peanut leaned against the wall, arms wrapped around herself, face pale with exhaustion. Victor remained alert, standing just behind her, eyes darting at every creak and flutter from the city waking up around them.

"Why wait until tomorrow?" Victor asked. "If they're going to seize power, why not do it now?"

Alric's voice was low, almost a growl. "Because they want to appear legitimate. They'll claim unity. Stability. They'll dress up a coup as the noble work of statesmen."

He paused, scanning the alley's mouth before continuing.

"Hobbs will be there. So will Chancellor Tovik, General Rell, and others. If we're going to stop this, we can't just catch another assassin. We have to expose the head of the beast. In front of witnesses."

Peanut brushed a hand over her eyes. "And you want us there?"

"I can get you in. Disguised. I'll vouch for you both. But it's dangerous—more than anything yet."

Victor sighed. "We're already in this far."

Peanut nodded. "We're with you."

Alric allowed a faint smile. "Good. Then tonight, we move. But first—get some rest. The sun's coming up. Shalonai knows we'll need our strength."

By the time Peanut and Victor slipped out of the alley, dawn had stretched across the city. The ocean glowed like molten gold, and the air carried the scent of salt and ash. The docks were stirring—quietly, cautiously—as if the harbor itself sensed something was wrong.

They wound through narrow lanes and crooked walkways, finally reaching the berth of the Windrat.

The pirate ship swayed gently in the morning tide, its patched sails bundled like old parchment. Sump was already on deck, whistling tunelessly as he hammered a splintered board into place.

Victor muttered, "Does he ever sleep?"

"Not since the lantern fire incident, I think," Peanut replied, managing a weary smile.

From the quarterdeck, a broad figure stepped into the sun. Mossback squinted down at them, his thick arms folded, his jaw set.

"Well, I'll be," the old turtle rumbled. "You two look like you've been through the wringer."

Peanut offered a tired wave. "Morning, Captain. The city's in chaos. The king's dead. We don't have anywhere else safe to go."

Victor added, "We were hoping we could stay here. Just until things settle."

Mossback raised a jagged brow. "You didn't have anything to do with the king dying, did you?" His voice was slow, gravelly. "I'd hate for rumors to start that I'm harboring royal assassins. Bad for business."

There was a long silence.

Then Mossback barked a laugh. "Relax. I'm only half-serious. You can stay as long as you need—just don't make a habit of bringing coups to my deck."

Peanut gave him a grateful nod. "Thank you."

"Cabin's open. Find a corner and crash."

They boarded the Windrat. The old ship creaked and groaned, but it felt like home. Or close enough to it for now.

Peanut slumped against a barrel just inside the cabin door. Sleep took her before she could even kick off her boots. Victor stayed beside her, watching the sun rise over the sea.

Tomorrow, they would face the council.

Tonight, they slept.

Peanut woke with her face mashed into something damp and her mouth dry as sand. She blinked blearily and pushed herself up, only to realize there was a long string of drool connecting her cheek to the wooden floor.

"Ugh," she muttered, wiping it away with her sleeve.

The cabin was quiet except for the creak of the Windrat's hull and the distant cry of gulls. Sunlight streamed through the cracks in the boards—far too bright. Judging by the heat and angle, it was well past noon.

She stumbled upright and pushed the door open, blinking into the warm, salty air of the top deck.

"'Bout time you joined the land of the living," cackled Polly from behind a large pot hung over a fire near the mast. The parrot wore an apron far too big for her frame and stirred with a wooden spoon nearly her height. Whatever was bubbling in the pot smelled like roasted peppers, onions, and something savory Peanut couldn't quite place—but her stomach growled loudly enough to answer for her.

Victor lounged in the shade nearby, shirt tossed over his shoulder, chatting lazily with Sump, who was working on rigging with one hand and chewing a toothpick with the other. Mossback was nowhere in sight—probably napping in the helm room or brooding in a hammock.

They all sat together to eat—some kind of spicy vegetable stew with crusty bread that Polly swore "won't kill ya, promise." For a while, the mood was light. There was laughter. Stories. Sump told a wildly inaccurate tale about fighting off ten harbor guards with a single mop, and even Victor cracked a real smile.

But the warmth never quite reached Peanut's chest.

She picked at her food more than she ate it. Every time someone laughed too hard, it reminded her of Kip's laugh—quiet, quick, with that little hiccup at the end. She kept seeing his face behind bars, alone in the dark, probably trying to be brave. Probably scared.

She didn't say anything. Just let the food go cold.

As the afternoon drifted toward dusk and the stew pot was scraped clean, Peanut found herself wandering to the ship's edge.

She sat on the starboard side, feet dangling above the gentle lap of the water, staring out across the endless horizon. The sun sank slow and gold into the ocean, painting the sky in fire and peach. The salt wind brushed her fur, and she took a deep breath, trying to still the anxious gnawing in her chest.

Somewhere beneath that sky, under stone and torchlight, Kip was waiting. And tomorrow night, they'd make their move.

She watched the sun vanish and whispered under her breath:

"Hold on, Kip. We're coming."

The sea was calm, and the sky slowly faded from gold to violet. Peanut didn't move from her perch at the edge of the *Windrat*, her feet swinging gently above the water.

The sound of paws on wood drew her attention just enough to glance back. Victor eased down beside her with a sigh, arms draped loosely over his knees.

They sat in silence for a while, watching the last rays of sunlight shimmer across the ocean.

"I used to hate sunsets," Victor said quietly.

Peanut raised an eyebrow. "That's dramatic."

He chuckled, but there was no humor in it. "Yeah. Well. I think it was because every one felt like another day gone. Another day not knowing."

She didn't ask. She didn't need to.

Victor continued. "I was ten when the war hit my village. I got separated from my mum in the chaos—there were fires, shouting, everyone running... I just remember waking up on the road and being picked up by a Peacebound scout a few days later. They brought me to the Hollow. Said it was safer."

He let out a breath through his nose.

"I stayed. Grew up there. Trained. Fought. And all the while I kept thinking she was still out there, y'know? That she was looking for me just like I was looking for her." He paused, voice suddenly thinner. "But I never found her. And the worst part was, I don't know if I ever will. Or if she's even alive."

The quiet that followed was heavy. Peanut swallowed, her throat suddenly dry.

"I'm sorry," she murmured.

Victor shrugged, but his eyes were far away.

Peanut stared down at the waves. "That... actually hits close to home." She drew her knees up, hugging them to her chest. "There's a lady named Miss Tilda. She raised me and Kip after our parents were gone. We were safe. She loved us." She paused. "And then we just... left. We joined Varrin's army. We didn't even say goodbye. I left a note. A note."

Victor turned to look at her but said nothing.

"I thought I was being brave. Thought I was doing the right thing." She bit her lip. "But now I just feel like I ran off and broke her heart."

They sat there together, two small silhouettes against the vastness of the sea and sky, bound by silence and sorrow.

The deck creaked under a massive weight.

Suddenly the *Windrat* tilted just slightly, and Mossback settled down on Peanut's other side with the grace of a falling boulder.

The ship rocked with his arrival, and Peanut had to catch herself from sliding.

"Phew," Mossback groaned, patting his shell. "Hope I didn't tip us over. We still floatin'?"

Victor snorted, and Peanut managed a faint smile.

Mossback stared out at the sunset, his eyes half-lidded under his mossy brow. "Heard you two talkin'. Don't worry, wasn't eavesdroppin'. Just happened to be nearby. Real quiet-like. Like a leaf in the wind."

Victor raised a brow. "You creak like a wagon when you walk."

"I'm workin' on that."

There was a beat.

"I never knew my mother," Mossback said. "That's just how it was for turtles. Hatch out of an egg, and if you're lucky you don't get eaten by a gull. Never met her. Don't know what she looked like. Don't even know if she made it to the water."

Peanut turned to him, expecting a joke—but Mossback's face was oddly serene.

"But sometimes, when the sun sets like this," he continued, "I like to think she's out there somewhere, watchin' the same sunset. Maybe sittin' on a rock with a shell just like mine. Probably bigger. That's where I get it from."

He paused, then added, "Or maybe she was eaten by a heron. But that's less comfortin', so I stick with the rock idea."

Victor burst into a laugh, shaking his head.

Peanut laughed too, though a tear snuck from the corner of her eye and she wiped it away quickly.

Mossback stretched, joints popping like tree branches in the wind. "Anyway, we all got ghosts, don't we? What matters is what we do with the time we've got. And who we spend it with." He gave them a knowing glance. "Now get some more rest if you can. Big night ahead. Spies and secret meetings and probably a whole lotta running."

He pushed himself up and waddled away, the *Windrat* groaning in protest beneath him.

Victor leaned back on his elbows. "I like him."

Peanut watched Mossback go, then turned her eyes back to the sea. "Yeah," she said softly. "Me too."

The *Windrat* swayed gently with the rhythm of the tide, moored quietly in the harbor as a warm evening wind brushed across its weathered sails. From the shore, the ship looked half-asleep, lanterns glowing softly along the railing, a single seagull perched on the bowsprit, preening in the last golden light of day.

Peanut tightened the strap across her shoulder. The satchel, worn thin and patched in places, bumped against her hip with each step. Her fur still smelled faintly of Polly's afternoon stew—a bittersweet comfort as she and Victor stood on the dock once again, preparing to walk back into danger.

"You sure you're up for this?" Victor asked, glancing sideways at her. His voice was low, a steady counter to the rising sounds of the evening city. "You didn't sleep much. And I'm pretty sure I saw you drooling on your cloak."

Peanut gave a tired smile. "Thanks for the reminder."

He shrugged. "Just trying to keep things grounded."

From the gangplank, Mossback approached. The old turtle moved slowly, each step deliberate, as though weighed down not only by his shell but by the years he'd carried it. He stopped in front of them, arms crossed, the tip of his beak catching the glint of the harbor lights.

"You two," he said simply.

Peanut nodded. "We'll be careful."

Mossback raised a scaly brow. "You always say that right before diving headfirst into trouble."

Polly landed on the railing behind him with a flutter of wings. "If you don't come back, I'm eating your stew rations," she chirped.

Victor smirked. "If we don't come back, you can have my hammock too. It's the one that doesn't creak."

"Liar," Polly snorted. "They all creak."

Sump appeared from below deck, still in his patched work vest, wiping oil off his paws with a rag. He didn't say anything—just gave a little salute with his greasy fingers.

Mossback studied them both for a long moment. Then he huffed.

"You bring any trouble back here," he said, "just make sure it's the kind that can't swim."

Peanut chuckled. "Got it."

Victor grinned. "We'll see you soon."

Mossback turned without another word, lumbering back toward the ship, while Polly gave them a jaunty wave. The *Windrat* faded behind them as they slipped into the twisting streets of the city once more.

Night blanketed the city in deep shadows and amber torchlight. The streets were mostly quiet, save for the occasional patrol or the distant clatter of a cart being wheeled home. In the far distance, the guttural rumble of unrest still simmered—echoes of a kingdom shaken by the death of its king.

Peanut and Victor moved with purpose, cloaks drawn up, sticking to the edges of alleys and broken fences. They wound their way through the lower tiers of the city, eventually arriving at the old watchtower—a crumbling relic from centuries past that leaned awkwardly near the edge of the western wall.

Sir Alric was already there, waiting in the dark beneath the tower's shadow. The greyhound's dark cloak made him nearly invisible until he shifted and the moonlight caught the steel of his belt buckle.

"Right on time," he said quietly.

Victor raised a brow. "You're sure this isn't some clever way to walk us into a dungeon cell?"

Alric gave a dry snort. "If I wanted you imprisoned, you'd be snoring in irons by now."

Peanut folded her arms. "So, how exactly were we getting in?"

Alric gestured with his head. "Follow me."

Behind the tower was a rusted gate that led to a disused storage yard—crates rotted to mush, old barrels eaten through with mold. Alric moved aside a stack of debris and revealed a small iron grate embedded in the ground.

He pulled it open with a creak that made all three of them wince, then gestured toward a narrow stone stairwell descending into darkness.

"Welcome to the back door," he muttered. "Old smuggling route from before the city grew this high. Comes out just below the central prison level. I've used it once or twice. Nobody else even remembers it's here."

Peanut peered into the dark, nose twitching. "Great. Another tunnel."
Victor rolled his eyes and started down. "Better than the sewers."

They descended slowly, the air damp and cool around them. The passage was narrow, barely wide enough for two to walk side by side, the walls of aged stone slick with condensation. Faint sounds echoed from above—distant city noise fading behind them.

As they walked, Alric spoke in a hushed tone.

"The meeting's supposed to be deep in the dungeon's lower levels. Council members only. But if Ironfang's message was convincing enough, they'll all be there."

Peanut frowned. "And you think someone's going to reveal themselves?"

"I hope so," Alric replied. "But I'm more interested in who doesn't."

They rounded a bend and came to another iron gate—this one slightly ajar. Beyond it, the passage opened into a larger, cleaner hallway lit by old oil lamps. Murals were carved into the walls here—remnants of some ceremonial chamber long forgotten. This was no prison corridor; it was older, secretive, and likely reserved for meetings meant to be hidden.

Voices echoed faintly from further ahead. Footsteps. A rhythmic tapping, like a cane or walking stick.

Alric held up a hand, motioning them to silence. They ducked into a recess in the wall just as a tall goose, cloaked in high-ranking robes, strode past them, grumbling under his breath. He moved with the kind of pride that didn't expect ambush, disappearing around the corner.

The three of them waited a beat, then crept forward after him.

Alric nodded toward the edge of the passage. "We'll watch from there. Just beyond that turn is the inner chamber. Once we're close enough, keep quiet. Don't move unless I say."

They inched forward. From where they crouched, they could see flickers of lamplight and shifting shadows as more figures gathered. One voice—the goose's—rose above the rest.

"What is this about?" he asked someone unseen. "Who called this meeting? I was told it was urgent—something about the future of the city."

Peanut's ears perked up. She glanced at Alric, then Victor. They were both tense, brows furrowed.

Another voice answered—a marmot, by the sound. "I received the same summons. No name. Just a seal."

"Ironfang," the goose muttered.

The name hung in the air like smoke.

Peanut's breath caught.

They didn't know.

Chapter 24

A Whisper Too Loud

From their dark corner of the corridor, Peanut, Victor, and Alric stayed perfectly still. Just beyond the stone archway, the inner chamber of the dungeon flickered with torchlight. Robed figures moved within, murmuring in low voices—uneasy, disjointed.

The goose, tall and rigid, stood near the center of the chamber, flanked by a marmot who clutched a leather folder to his chest.

"I don't understand," the goose said sharply. "My message said this meeting was urgent. Matters of national safety. But there's no seal, no signature. Just a wax stamp with some—some... fang?"

The marmot shook his head. "Same here. No official directive. The letter told me to come to the old dungeon at midnight. I thought it was a mistake."

Another voice—older, scratchier—chimed in from a weasel near the back. "This was improper protocol. No guard escort. No public record. This wasn't scheduled in the ledger."

"Then who called us here?" the goose demanded, voice rising.

Victor glanced at Alric. "They don't know who summoned them."

Alric's face was tense. "No one did."

More council members trickled in—an anxious badger, a sharp-eyed fox, a portly newt—each one exchanging confused glances, asking the same questions. Why were they called? Who else was coming? Where was the chairperson? The silence only fueled their nerves.

"This was a trap," Alric whispered.

Victor nodded slowly. "A real elaborate one."

Peanut's stomach twisted. "But why? And by who?"

Inside the chamber, the marmot stepped forward hesitantly. "There was a name on the letter," he said. "Ironfang. Do any of you know it?"

A long pause.

"Ironfang?" The goose scoffed. "Sounds like something from a nursery tale."

"No one on the council uses a title like that," said the fox, suspicious.

Before anyone could speak further, a loud slam echoed from the far end of the room—not from the passage where Peanut's group hid, but from a second entrance behind the chamber.

A rush of armored guards flooded in—dozens of them, moving with coordination and grim resolve. They spread like wildfire through the chamber, cutting off every exit. Cloaks and boots swirled in the torchlight.

Peanut clamped a paw over her mouth.

"Hold fast!" the goose shouted, startled. "State your purpose!"

A tall badger stepped to the front of the guards. His armor was darker than the rest, edged in crimson. He held up a rolled scroll and spoke with authority.

"By order of the High Command, all present members of the Council are hereby placed under arrest for conspiracy against the throne."

Chaos erupted.

The marmot dropped his folder. The weasel stumbled backward. The badger councilor growled, "What conspiracy? This is madness!"

"This is treason," hissed the lead guard. "And your reckoning has come."

"No!" the fox barked. "This isn't right. We haven't even met—this isn't sanctioned!"

Guards grabbed them one by one, binding their paws, silencing their protests. No one resisted for long. There were too many. Too fast.

Victor leaned in, whispering, "They're executing an order—but not one from the real council. This was staged. Preplanned."

"Then who's really giving the orders?" Peanut asked, her voice tight.

Alric stared, as though trying to read the answer in the torchlight.

"Whoever Ironfang was... they're not one of them. This wasn't a meeting. It was bait."

In the chamber, the marmot finally cried out, "Who's behind this? Who do you serve?!"

The lead guard didn't flinch. "The one who saw through your lies. The one who brings the reckoning."

His voice echoed off the stone.

Then, a whisper—one voice, perhaps a guard's, perhaps not—muttered just loud enough to carry:

"Long live Ironfang."

The name hung in the air like smoke.

Peanut's breath caught. She looked to Victor, then Alric. None of them spoke. No one knew what they'd just witnessed.

The guards began dragging the councilors out, one by one. No formal charges. No trials. No explanations.

Just silence.

And confusion.

Victor stepped back from the wall. "We need to leave."

Alric nodded, eyes still fixed on the chamber. "Someone's rewriting the rules. And none of us know who's holding the pen."

Peanut swallowed, her mind racing. "Ironfang... whoever that was... just took down the council without showing their face."

And for the first time since entering the city, none of them had the faintest idea what came next.

The tunnels behind them, Peanut, Victor, and Alric stepped out into the cool night air. The city's streets were quiet at this hour, lit only by scattered lanterns swaying in the breeze. Above, clouds drifted across the moon like slow-moving ships.

None of them spoke for a while.

Peanut inhaled deeply. "So that really just happened."

Alric's jaw tightened. "Half the council, arrested like common thieves. Without explanation. Without a leader giving the command."

Victor shook his head. "And no one knew who Ironfang was. Not even the ones who showed up."

They moved cautiously through the side alleys, sticking to the shadows as they made their way back toward the harbor. Every noise made Peanut's ears twitch. Her tail flicked behind her with nervous energy. It was too quiet now.

"What do we do next?" she asked softly.

Alric glanced around. "First, we get back to the boat. Regroup. Find out what's happening in the upper districts. That many arrests won't stay quiet for long."

Victor muttered, "Nothing stays quiet in a city like this. Not for long."

They were just approaching a narrow intersection near the market square when footsteps echoed on the cobblestones. The three froze. A group of guards rounded the corner ahead—four of them, clad in city armor, moving with purpose.

Victor stepped closer to Peanut. Alric lowered his stance, hand resting on the hilt of his blade.

"Be ready," he said quietly.

The guards saw them. One in front—a young ferret with a short sword at his hip—sprinted forward, waving an arm.

"Sir Alric!" he called out. "Sir Alric, wait!"

The tension coiled tighter. Peanut's paw drifted toward her satchel. Victor already had one blade halfway drawn.

"Your presence is requested at the castle," the ferret said, slowing to a halt before them, panting slightly.

Alric narrowed his eyes. "By whose authority?"

The ferret swallowed. "Sir, I don't know the full story. I just heard the council members uncovered the names of King Bramble's killers. They sent word for you. As his friend... I figured you'd want to know."

Alric stood silent a beat longer, studying the guard's face. Then he nodded once, curt and controlled.

"Yes," he said. "Thank you. I shall go there at once."

The guards saluted. Without another word, they turned and disappeared down a side path, boots clacking on the stones.

As soon as they were out of sight, Victor exhaled. "That was close."

Peanut lowered her shoulders slightly. "Do you think they really know who did it?"

"I think," Alric replied, "that someone wants us at the castle tonight."

Victor frowned. "That could be a trap."

"It could be," Alric said. "But if someone was pulling strings... we won't find them hiding in shadows."

He glanced at the tall spires of the castle, looming in the distance against the starlit sky.

"I think it's time," he said, "we met this Ironfang."

Peanut nodded slowly. Her heart thumped in her chest. She didn't know what waited for them inside those walls—but something was building. Something dark. Twisted.

They walked on in silence, the three of them, cloaks stirring gently in the wind.

Toward the castle.

Toward the truth.

Toward Ironfang.

The great doors of the castle creaked open with a deep groan, and Alric, Victor, and Peanut stepped inside.

Though it was long past midnight, the halls were alive with movement. Lanterns blazed from every column and archway, casting warm golden light across a sea of robes, armor, and confusion. Council members shuffled in from side doors and outer corridors, some yawning, some whispering anxiously. A few were still in nightgowns and slippers, having been roused from their beds without warning.

A pair of guards hurried past, escorting a groggy-looking fox who clutched a cloak over his bedclothes. The fox muttered something about treason and complained under his breath.

Peanut stuck close to Victor as they navigated the crowd, trying not to get separated. The air felt electric—every conversation a hushed speculation, every face tight with unease.

Suddenly, Peanut bumped into someone.

"Oh—sorry!" she blurted, stepping back.

Before her stood an elegant, elderly swan draped in silver and violet robes, her feathers speckled with age. Her long neck curved gracefully as she turned to look at Peanut. A soft smile played on her beak.

"No harm done, child," she said warmly, her voice a gentle hush beneath the chaos. "It's easy to lose your bearings on a night like this."

Peanut looked up at her. "Do you... do you know what's going on?"

The swan folded her wings slowly, eyes glinting with quiet wisdom. "Not yet. But history was often full of chaos in the moment. Only later did we begin to see the threads clearly. What we call 'truth' was so often stitched together long after the facts have faded."

There was a strange calmness to her. A certainty that made Peanut pause.

"What's your name?" Peanut asked.

"I am Lady Corvina of Greydown," she replied. "Royal historian to the Hollow Throne. And—though few know it—Keeper of the Testament."

Peanut tilted her head. "Testament?"

Corvina chuckled softly. "A story for another time, dear."

She turned, her eyes sweeping across the growing crowd of council members—stoats, badgers, birds, mice—all gathering beneath the vaulted ceiling like anxious birds before a storm.

"Whatever happens tonight," Corvina murmured, "I suspect it will be written in the pages of history. The only question is... whose version will survive?"

Before Peanut could respond, a trumpet blared, high and sharp, cutting through the noise like a blade. All eyes turned toward the staircase.

Descending with practiced poise came Master Hobbs, the Master-at-Arms and second only to the king in matters of war. The old pug wore a ceremonial tunic embroidered with the Hollow's seal, his every movement deliberate and dignified.

"Good evening, esteemed council," Hobbs said as he reached the marble floor. His voice was gravelly but strong, carrying easily across the chamber.

"I thank you for your swift arrival. I know this summons was sudden, but tonight, grave matters must be addressed. Please, take your seats."

The crowd began to shift toward the inner hall, murmuring as they went. Corvina offered Peanut a small nod, then glided away like a ghost in moonlight.

Victor leaned in to whisper, “I don’t like this. Feels like something’s about to snap.”

Peanut nodded, her eyes drifting toward the double doors of the high chamber. Behind them, something waited.

Truth... or deception.

And somewhere, watching from the shadows...

Ironfang.

Chapter 25

Trapped in the Jaws

The high chamber of the castle pulsed with quiet tension. Flames from hanging lanterns cast long shadows across the stone walls as Master Hobbs stepped forward, his boots striking firmly against the polished floor. He was dressed not in his usual soldier's garb, but in a crisp ceremonial coat—deep crimson with golden trim—the kind only worn by those who knew their words would shape the future.

"Councilors of Marrathil," he began, voice carrying without strain. "I thank you for coming, especially at such a late hour. But I assure you—what I have to say could not wait until dawn."

Sleepy-eyed council members, many still in house robes and nightcoats, shifted uncomfortably on the benches. Whispers died down. Even the fire seemed to still.

"As many of you know, King Bramble was a friend to me. I served under him, fought beside him. He was a patient ruler—wise and cautious—but not blind."

Hobbs paused.

"In his final weeks, King Bramble confided in me his deepest suspicion: that his brother's death was no accident. And worse—that his own life was in danger as well."

A ripple of shock moved through the room. Several council members turned to each other, mouths slightly agape.

Peanut stood quietly near the edge of the chamber beside Alric and Victor, half-hidden behind a pillar. None of them spoke—but each felt the slow prickle of tension tightening in their chests.

"I knew the danger of making open accusations," Hobbs continued. "The council was large, respected. To move recklessly could throw Marrathil into panic—or worse, civil war."

He took a breath and stepped forward.

"So I waited. I listened. And when the time came, I infiltrated a hidden meeting beneath the city—a gathering of those who plotted against the crown." He held up a sealed scroll, hand trembling slightly.

"With one swift strike, my loyal guards moved in. We apprehended every traitor present. They now sit in the dungeons, awaiting their judgment."

Gasps echoed through the room. Dozens of eyes darted around the council chamber. Many sat frozen. A few shook their heads in stunned silence.
Peanut's tail twitched. "He really found them..." she whispered under her breath.
Victor, arms crossed, muttered, "Or he wants us to believe he did."
Alric said nothing, gaze fixed on Hobbs with a soldier's calm—calculating, waiting.

"I regret to inform you," Hobbs went on, "that the traitors were not from outside these walls. They were among you."

Another gasp. The chamber began to murmur—some councilors rising to their feet, others shrinking in disbelief.

"They sought to remove King Bramble because he refused to join the war," Hobbs said. "They saw him as weak, as a hindrance to King Varrin's ambitions. And so they took gold from our enemies—bribes, promises of power."

The weight of the accusation sank in hard. For all the chaos the war had brought, few had imagined such betrayal could rise from the heart of Marrathil's own leadership.
One gray-furred badger near the back shouted, "Names! Who among us betrayed the king?"

Hobbs raised a steady hand. "Their names will be revealed once the trials begin. Until then, know this: the rot has been cut away... but some roots may remain."
Uneasy murmurs swelled again. Suspicion crept like a draft through the room.

"And now," Hobbs said, voice rising, "with both Jorm and Thorim dead, and the council shaken to its core, we must act. We must act not with delay or fear, but with resolve—for the sake of Marrathil's future, and for its very survival."
He looked out across the sea of troubled faces.
"Dawn is coming. But whether it brings peace or ruin... depends on what we choose now."
From the shadows, Peanut could feel the air thicken. Not with answers.
But with a hundred more questions.

Master Hobbs stood tall in the center of the chamber, the soft torchlight glinting off the gold trim of his uniform. Around him, the murmuring council began to settle as he raised his voice once more.

"The council is fractured," he said solemnly. "The bloodline of the kings has ended. Were we in gentler times, we might have had the luxury of mourning. Of healing. Of rebuilding."

He let the silence sit heavy for a moment.

"But these are not such times. Chaos will hit the streets by sunrise if the people discover that not only is their king dead... but that he was slain by the very council meant to protect him."

He scanned the faces before him, pausing to meet the eyes of each gathered noble.

"Either Varnack or Varrin could march through our gates by week's end. And if that happens, with no king, no unity—we will not have the strength to stop them."

He took a step forward, his voice rising in passion.

"Marrathil has long been a bastion of peace and light. An oasis in the chaos of war. We must preserve it. And to do that... the city must not wake to a power vacuum. We must crown a new king. Tonight."

A wave of alarm rippled through the chamber. Dozens of eyes turned to each other, uncertain and searching.

Alric leaned close to Victor and whispered, "This is moving far too quickly."

Victor frowned. "Feels like it was always meant to."

Peanut just stared, heart thudding, unsure if she was watching a city saved... or stolen.

Hobbs raised his hand. "To ensure transparency, I call upon the Royal Historian to recite the laws of succession."

A hush fell as a swan stepped forward from the edge of the crowd. Dressed in flowing violet robes, her long white feathers swayed with grace. She moved slowly but with an undeniable dignity, her piercing eyes scanning the room.

"Lady Corvina," Hobbs announced. "You carry the knowledge of our city's founding. Please, enlighten us."

Corvina paused in the center of the circle, illuminated beneath the stained-glass skylight overhead. She looked not at Hobbs, but at the council.

"History," she said, her voice calm and measured, "was written in ink... but it is lived in blood."

A hush hung on her words.

"Few times in our city's long memory has the royal line ended," she continued. "And never under such vile and tangled circumstances. The death of King Bramble—like that of his brother—will scar the stones of this city for generations to come."

She turned, looking out at all assembled.

"I urge you all, in this fragile moment, to proceed with wisdom and restraint. The decisions we make tonight—"

"With all respect, Historian," Hobbs cut in, voice sharp. "We asked you to cite precedent, not deliver a sermon on patience."

A stiff silence followed. Corvina's beak tightened. She turned back toward the council, her voice colder now.

"Very well," she said. "According to the Treaties of Unification, signed at the ratification of Marrathil, should the king die without a rightful heir, then the Council of Elders shall elect a new monarch from among the noble families—but only with a full quorum present."

She glanced pointedly at the many empty seats.

Hobbs didn't miss a beat. "And unfortunately, with half the council rotting in the dungeons, and others suspected of treason, a quorum is... impossible."

He turned to the room, raising his voice.

"And with both foreign armies moving ever closer, I declare that Marrathil is in a state of war."

Gasps erupted. Several councilors rose to protest, but Corvina raised her wing. The room quieted again.

Her eyes narrowed into cold steel.
"If the bloodline ends," she said, "and the city is in a declared state of war..."
A beat passed.
"Then, by law, the kingship passes to the Master at Arms."
The words hung in the air like a guillotine blade.
"To you, Master Hobbs."
A breathless silence followed.
And somewhere in the dark corner of the chamber, Peanut felt her stomach twist.
Victor muttered, "Well. That explains everything."

Peanut stood frozen beside Victor and Alric as the murmurs began.

Around the grand chamber, the surviving council members exchanged wary glances. Their eyes darted, searching one another's faces, trying to gauge guilt or innocence—trust unraveling with every heartbeat. The weight of treason hung heavy in the air, infecting even the uninvolved with suspicion.

Victor leaned in close to Peanut. "This is it. He's done it. They're all too shaken to stop him."

Alric stepped forward, hands clenched at his sides. His voice rang out clear, cutting through the tense quiet.

"I served King Bramble for twenty years," he said. "Not just as his guard... not just as his general. He was my dearest friend. A better man than I ever was. And though these are dark and uncertain days, I know this—Bramble would never want this city to tear itself apart because of his death. He would want us to stand firm. To show the world that Marrathil endures."
Before Alric could continue, Hobbs cut in, loud and commanding:

"Exactly!" he boomed. "We must not be weak in these times. If we fail to act—if we hesitate now—then we betray the memory of both King Brambles. We must unite. Tonight. Not for ourselves, but to honor the kings we lost."

The words barely had time to land before a gray-furred wolf councilor stood abruptly.

"I agree!" he called. "I propose we crown Hobbs king!"

A silence followed—brief, stunned.

Then, like a dam breaking, the chamber erupted.

"Unheard of!"

"This is madness!"

"You cannot be serious!"

"He's grabbing power!"

But above the shouting, louder than any protest, came a swelling chant from the back corner of the chamber:

"Hobbs for king! Hobbs for king!"

The chant grew, louder and bolder, catching like wildfire.

"Long live King Hobbs! Long live King Hobbs!"

Peanut looked around in horror as more and more voices joined in—some shouting with conviction, others just trying to be on the winning side.

Alric stood motionless amid the storm, dismay etched across his face.

"This isn't right," Victor muttered, fists clenched.

Peanut couldn't take it anymore. She ran forward, trying to push past the guards, trying to be heard over the noise.

"Wait! Please—listen!" she shouted. "This can't be how it ends! You're being—"

But no one listened. Her voice vanished into the rising sea of cheers.

Hobbs raised both hands.

And the chamber fell silent.

He looked around with practiced solemnity, eyes resting briefly on each councilor... then on Alric... and finally on Peanut.

"It seems," Hobbs said slowly, "that our council is in agreement."

He turned to the throne behind him, its gilded frame catching the flicker of torchlight.

"With these trying times upon us," he said, "I accept the role of king with great humility. I do this not for power... but for the survival of Marrathil."

The chamber erupted in applause.

"I promise you—I will steer our city through the turbulent storm we now face. And when we emerge, we will be stronger than ever before!"

Cheers.

"We will be richer! More united! More glorious!"

Louder cheers.

"And the whole world will look upon our banners... and tremble! For we will drive back both armies and show them what Marrathil is made of!"

The chamber shook with applause and stomping feet as Hobbs turned, ascended the final steps, and lowered himself onto the throne.

A hush fell.

The roar vanished as quickly as it had come.

And in that quiet, Hobbs looked down—his gaze falling on the small squirrel girl standing at the edge of the circle, eyes wide, chest heaving.

His expression softened. He gave a slow, pitiful smile.

"And what greater way to begin my reign," he said, "than with an act of mercy."

He stood and pointed toward her.

"Peanut," he called. "Come forward."

Chapter 26

Defanged

Peanut's steps echoed faintly across the marble floor as she approached the throne. The room held its breath.

Hobbs leaned forward in his seat—majestic, towering, cloaked in authority, but wearing the mask of kindness.

"Peanut," he said, his voice warm, sorrowful. "I know you and your companions were innocent in the matter of King Bramble's death."

A murmur swept through the chamber.

"I'm sorry you were caught in this storm. Children should never be dragged into the business of betrayal and blood." He rose from the throne, spreading his arms wide. "And so—my first act as your king is to pardon you. You, and your friends. All charges are lifted."

A thunderous cheer broke out. Council members clapped, some dabbing their eyes as if moved by the new king's mercy. Even Victor shifted uneasily beside Alric, uncertain what to believe anymore.

Peanut blinked, stunned—but not with relief.

She looked up at Hobbs.

Her voice came quiet, unsteady, but clear. "There's a conspiracy," she said, not shouting—just speaking truth. "It goes deeper than this council. Maybe deeper than this city. We didn't kill King Bramble—but I think we're standing in front of someone who helped."

The room turned sharp.

The gray-furred wolf from earlier slammed his paw against the table and rose.

"Enough!"

His voice sliced through the air like a blade. "This is a night for unity, not wild accusations! We have peace at last, and a new king to lead us. We will not spend it second-guessing our fortune just because a child was confused."

Cries of agreement rose quickly, angry and overwhelming.

"Enough talk!"

"The king has spoken!"

"Let it rest!"

Peanut's shoulders slumped. Her hands trembled.

She had lost.

In her mind's eye, she saw King Bramble—not long ago, smiling down at her and Kip like a father might. She remembered Kazik, his eyes shining with reverence whenever he spoke of the Bramble Kings.

They had been more than rulers. They were beacons.

And now...

Her eyes filled with tears.

She dropped to her knees before the throne—not in reverence, but in heartbreak.

The crowd misunderstood. They saw only a girl overcome by gratitude.

Cheers rose again:

"Hobbs the Merciful!"

"Long live the king!"

Hobbs descended the final step and knelt beside her, his voice low, for her ears alone.

"I don't know what you think you know, child," he murmured. "But it's over."

He extended his hand, heavy with jeweled rings.

"Come. Kiss my rings as a sign of respect and admiration. And this will all be over."

Peanut didn't move. Hot tears streaked down her face.

Kiss his rings?

The same rings worn by the man who had stolen the throne? The one who dared to play the part of peacemaker while cloaked in treachery?

She looked down at his hand, fury stirring deep in her chest.

Six rings—three on each hand. Most were gaudy, gleaming with polished stones. But one was different.

Plain. Silver.

A signet ring.

Etched with a single mark:

A wolf... biting into a crown.

Her heart stopped.

She'd seen that sigil before.

On the letter Victor had stolen from the Baroness's study. The seal that marked the first whisper of betrayal.

The same mark tied to the name Ironfang.
Peanut stared at the ring.
She didn't need anyone to explain it.
She knew.

Peanut stared at the signet ring—its cruel emblem seared into her memory. Her breath caught, heart pounding.

Then, without thinking, she lunged.

Her paw closed around Hobbs' hand. He jerked back in surprise, stumbling. The weight of the moment—and the girl's sudden defiance—threw him off balance. With a thud, the would-be king tumbled down the steps of the throne.

Gasps echoed through the chamber.

Peanut didn't hesitate. She climbed a few steps and turned to face the council, her voice ringing out like a bell in the silence.

"He's the murderer!" she cried. "Hobbs! He's the one who killed King Bramble!"

A murmur swept the room. Eyes turned. The fragile illusion shattered.

"We can prove it!"

She spun around. "Victor! The note!"

Victor, stunned but quick, shoved through the onlookers and sprinted toward her. Hobbs scrambled upright, his face twisted in rage.

"Guards!" he bellowed. "Arrest them! Now!"

From the edges of the hall, armored soldiers moved forward, spears raised.

But then—another voice rang out.

"Halt!"

Alric's voice, sharp and commanding, cut through the noise like a sword.

The guards froze mid-step.

Alric strode forward, calm but firm. "Hobbs has not been crowned. He is not king. Not yet. This council still stands—and I am still Commander of this city's guard."

The soldiers hesitated... then lowered their weapons.

Victor reached into his satchel and pulled out the weathered slip of parchment.

"The Baroness was part of it," he said, loud enough to reach every corner. "This note was found in her quarters. It carries the same symbol—"

Peanut grabbed Hobbs' hand again. "Then let's see what's hiding behind your mercy."

Hobbs shrieked and thrashed, but Peanut yanked the ring free.

"YIIPP!" he howled, clutching his fingers. "You little—!"

Peanut held up the ring. A simple silver band. Etched with a single mark.

A wolf. Biting a crown.

Victor raised the note beside it.

The two marks were identical.

Silence.

Alric stepped forward, took both items from their hands, and studied them. Slowly, others approached—councilors, guards, officials. One by one, they looked.

Gasps. Murmurs. Cries.

"Traitor!"

"He planned it all!"

"He killed the king!"

"He lied to us!"

A ripple of outrage surged through the chamber. Some surged forward, faces twisted with fury.

"Let us tear him apart!" roared the wolf councilor, now wild-eyed. "He used us!"

But Alric raised a hand.

"No."

His voice was clear. Final.

"We are not like him."

He turned to the guards. "Take him to the dungeon. He will face judgment."

Two soldiers moved in. Hobbs flailed and kicked as they dragged him toward the doors, frothing with desperation.

"I'm Innocent! Innocent! They're lying! Don't listen to them! I AM YOUR KING!"

But no one listened.

The doors opened. Then slammed shut.

And Hobbs was gone.

The chamber still hummed with the echoes of outrage and disbelief. One by one, the council members filed out—some in silence, others whispering as they went, disoriented, ashamed, or simply relieved. No one remained behind.

Sir Alric stepped forward, his voice low but steady, worn thin by the night.

"Enough for one night," he said. "Too much chaos. Too much emotion. No good decisions are made under such weight. We'll reconvene tomorrow—rested and clear-headed. There's still work ahead of us."

No one argued.

The last murmurs faded into the long corridors beyond, and the great doors closed with a soft, final hush.

Peanut, Victor, and Alric stood alone in the vastness of the high chamber.

Victor broke the silence. "We did it."

Alric didn't answer. His gaze had drifted—past the empty benches, past the throne itself. He stepped forward slowly, his boots silent against the polished floor.

He came to the throne and lifted a hand, brushing the armrest with his fingers, as if it might disappear. Then his eyes rose to the great painting that hung above—the portrait of King Bramble.

The Stag's white fur glowed faintly in the lanternlight. His expression was calm, strong, wise. He had been more than a ruler. He had been a symbol. A friend. A vision of what peace could look like.

"Yes, Victor," Alric said at last, still staring upward. "We did it."

Peanut watched him, her chest tight. She could see it in his posture—the way his shoulders rose and fell, holding back a tide of grief. He stood tall, but only just. The battle had been won, but it had carved something out of him.

Alric's hands slowly curled into fists.

Victor made to step forward, but Peanut placed a paw on his arm and shook her head gently.

Let him have this.

Alric moved closer to the painting. He stood beneath it for a long while, breathing slow and deep. Then, with a trembling hand, he reached up and touched the edge of the canvas.

His voice, when it came, was raw.

"All he wanted was peace. He wanted what was best for his people. For this city."

He swallowed hard.

"For him to die to the desires of small men... just seems... such a waste."

Tears streaked his fur and fell to the floor, silent as snow.

Peanut's voice was soft. "He was a good man."

Victor nodded. "The best."

Alric's eyes never left the painting. "He was, my friend."

At last, he turned. The pain hadn't left his face, but something steadier had returned—something quiet and resolute.

"Come," he said, a touch of warmth returning to his voice. "Let's get your friends out of that cell. And then, finally... the two of you can rest."

A weary smile broke across his muzzle.

"Shalonai knows... we all could use it."

The cell door creaked open.

"Peanut!"

"Kip!"

They collided in the center of the room, nearly toppling over from the force of their embrace. Kip wrapped his arms around her like he might never let go, and Peanut held him just as tightly. She felt his warmth, his shaking breath, the quiet sob that escaped as though he hadn't been able to breathe until now.

Behind them, Victor sauntered in, arms folded, a grin tugging at his face. "Well, look who's been lounging in a cozy little stone spa while I was out saving the kingdom."

Kip pulled back, blinking at him. "Sorry I missed the fun. How many villains did you punch?"

"Just one," Victor replied, lifting his chin. "But it was a very round villain. Required great effort."

Kip snorted, and Peanut laughed, the weight in her chest easing.

Orin stepped forward, her eyes dark and kind. "Thank you," she said simply. "Both of you. We trusted you to do the right thing... and you did."

Malik nodded beside her. "We believed in you."

Peanut blinked hard, her heart swelling at the words. *Trusted.* Orin had said it like it was never in question. That quiet certainty hit deeper than any praise. It left her throat tight.

They had believed in her.

She opened her mouth, but no words came—only a rush of emotion she couldn't name.

And then Malik pulled them all into a hug.

The great elephant wrapped his massive arms around the entire group, lifting them off the ground in one joyful squeeze. Kip squeaked. Victor yelped. Orin chuckled, her paws pinned. Peanut laughed and cried at the same time, pressed between warm fur, strong arms, and the safety of being known. Loved.

In that moment, wrapped in that awkward, wonderful embrace, something inside her settled.

She was Peacebound.

That night, for the first time in days, they sat around a real table and ate real food.

Kip and Orin tore into their meals like soldiers after battle. Kip devoured half a loaf of bread before noticing it had nuts in it—then kept going anyway. Orin plowed through her stew with the elegance of a wolf in a henhouse. Even Malik, normally so proper, slurped and munched with abandon, broth dribbling down his tusks.

Victor, amused, leaned over and offered Peanut a napkin with a gentleman's flourish.

They were safe. They were fed. They were together.

Later, in a quiet bunkroom above the kitchens, Peanut and Kip lay side by side in their small beds, wrapped in thin wool blankets. A single candle flickered low between them.

Kip rolled onto his side, voice soft. "You were amazing today. I mean it."

Peanut stared up at the ceiling. "We did what we had to do."

"Still," he murmured, "you stood up to a king. That's something."

She turned her head. "But Bramble's still gone. None of it brought him back. Nothing really got fixed."

Kip was quiet for a moment. Then, gently:

"Yeah. But... we can do the right thing again tomorrow. And the day after that."

He yawned, pulling the blanket closer.

"And little by little... we'll win."

Within seconds, his breathing slowed, deep and steady with sleep.

Peanut lay awake, watching the shadows on the wall. She wanted to believe him. Wanted to feel the victory they'd earned. But something heavy still clung to her chest—some things, even after justice, stayed broken.

She closed her eyes.

And waited for sleep that never came.

Chapter 27

Dawning Hope

The great doors of the throne room creaked open once more, this time not under fire or accusation, but quiet purpose.

Peanut, Kip, Orin, Malik, and Victor stepped inside, the morning sun filtering through the stained-glass windows in fractured colors. The air was cooler now, lighter somehow—yet beneath it still lingered the weight of everything that had come before.

Sir Alric stood by the dais, his armor polished, though his eyes looked older than yesterday.

"I wanted to see you before the council gathers," he said as they approached.

They gathered around him. Malik lowered himself gently to one knee beside them, his great frame taking up half the floor. Orin stood with her arms crossed, ever watchful. Peanut noticed how Victor leaned casually against a pillar, but even he seemed unusually quiet.

"I wanted to tell you," Alric began, voice solemn, "that after a full investigation, we have confirmed it. Hobbs was Ironfang."

Gasps spread among the group, even though they had all suspected it.

"He funded the assassins that murdered both King Thorim and King Jorm," Alric said. "And he nearly took the throne himself through lies, manipulation, and fear."

A long silence followed. Then Alric added, "We found the group of assassins he employed. Most of them. But the one known as The Baroness—she slipped away. Someone tipped her off before we arrived."

Peanut's stomach turned. Another traitor was still hiding. Another shadow.

"There were still conspirators in the council," Alric said darkly. "Hobbs couldn't have done this alone. He needed allies."

Kip stepped forward, frowning. "So what were you going to do about them? How will you find them? And what happens when you do?"

Alric's eyes met his.

"Their fangs have been pulled," he said coolly. "They're no threat for now. But lies... lies always rot from within. They will show themselves in time."

He turned and looked out at the hall.

"And when they do, justice will find them. Darkness can hide things for a while, but the truth—truth always comes to light."

Peanut nodded slowly, but another question was forming in her mind. She hesitated.

"What happens now?" she asked. "Who's going to be king?"

It was hard not to think of the Kingstone, of their mission, of what came next for the Peacebound. But she knew this moment—the city's future—was bigger than just her.

"That," said Alric, "was for the council to decide. Now that Hobbs and his fear mongering were gone, and the falsely accused council members have been freed, the full council can meet. They can choose a new ruler with wisdom and patience. No more rash decisions made out of fear."

Orin nodded, arms still crossed. "There's a reason patience was a virtue."

They all turned at the sound of the doors opening again behind them.

Click. Clack. Click.

Lady Corvina entered, her long dark feathers brushing the marble floor, elegant and poised as ever. A few other aides followed in silence, but she alone approached the throne.

Peanut immediately straightened. There was something different about her today. A gravity in her steps. A purpose.

"Lady Corvina," said Alric, surprised. "The council meeting isn't for another hour."

"I know," she said gently. "But I've come early... for you."

She extended a small folded parchment. "This was for you, Sir Alric. Something of great importance. Something... personal."

Alric reached out. His fingers froze midair.

He stared at the wax seal—pressed deep with the symbol of an acorn crown.

His breath caught.

It was Bramble's seal.

With trembling hands, Alric took the letter.

No one spoke. Even Victor stood still. Peanut watched his jaw tighten as the knight she once thought unshakable slowly broke the seal and unfolded the letter with reverence.

His eyes moved across the page. His lips parted slightly. A tremor passed through him like a storm cloud shifting overhead.

If you were reading this, then my fears have come true, and I too have been taken by the assassin's knife.

I want you to forgive yourself, my friend. There was nothing you could have done to stop it. Sometimes there are powers that move beyond our grasp, tides that turn no matter how we brace against them. And even though I know—without a doubt—that you would have given your own life to save mine, it was often not our choice to make.

You know I believe the council to be behind my brother's murder. You always doubted it, tried to see the good in them—but I ask you now to follow that suspicion, and discover the truth. I leave this not as a command, but as a plea from someone who trusted you with everything. I know your upbringing as a bloodhound will not allow you to lose the scent. So follow it. Find them. And bring justice back into this broken world.

What I ask of you now... was something I ask with a heavy heart.

I have no sons, as you well know. No heirs to carry my line. And I did not trust any noble family with the throne—not after what I've seen. But there was one I trust.

You.

I have named you my rightful heir.

Forgive me, Alric, for placing this burden on your shoulders. I know you never desired power. You never chased crowns or titles. But that was why you were the one who must wear it. It was always the ones who did not seek to rule who were most worthy of doing so.

Stay strong, old friend. Stay courageous. Do not be afraid to do what is right, even when it costs you everything. You have always been humble. You have always been kind. Those qualities were not weaknesses—they were the soul of good leadership.

Lead our people. Keep peace within our walls. Watch carefully, because the fingers of both Varrin and Varnack will seek every crack to enter the city. You

must not let them in—not through fear, not through compromise, not through pride.
And did not cry for me.

I served our people with all I had. Even unto death. I only ask now that you did the same. Serve them. Love them. Be the shield I can no longer be.
Goodbye, old friend.
—Thorim

Sir Alric stood in silence, the letter trembling in his paw. His eyes glistened, and though he did everything in his power to hold them back, a few tears slipped free, trailing down the fur of his worn cheeks.

The Peacebound watched him quietly. Peanut shifted on her feet, glancing at Kip, whose brow furrowed with unease. Was this more bad news? Another betrayal?

But Corvina stood still, her face composed. She watched not with sorrow... but with a quiet sort of peace. Like a weight she had carried alone had finally been passed on.

Alric finally lifted his gaze, voice low and thick. "You knew?"

Corvina nodded. "Of course I knew. I am the Keeper of the Testament. My duty is to preserve the final words and documents of the Hollow Throne. That letter... was among them."

He looked back down, staring at the folded parchment in his paw as though it might vanish.

"So it's real?" His voice cracked. "Thorim wanted me to be king?" He almost laughed, but it caught halfway up. "Why me?"

"I did not read the letter," Corvina said gently, stepping forward, "but King Thorim spoke of you often. He admired you, Alric. Trusted you. And I believe that letter explains exactly why he chose you for this."

Alric shook his head faintly. "I'm not ready. Someone else—someone wiser, someone with more—"

"There was no one else," Corvina said. Not harshly. Just truthfully. "You saw what fear did to the council. What ambition did to Hobbs. You saw how quickly people reached for power, not to serve—but to rule."

She met his eyes.

"You don't want the crown. That's exactly why it belongs to you."

Kip stepped forward, eyes wide. "Wait... wait, wait. You mean King Bramble wanted *you* to be king?"

"It appears so," Orin said evenly.

Peanut's eyes glowed, her voice soft. "I think you'll make a great king."

Victor grinned. "As long as you don't make us wear silly uniforms or bow every time you walk into the room, I'm all in."

A few chuckles stirred through the group. Even Kip smiled now, glancing at Alric with a new kind of respect.

But Alric didn't laugh. Not yet. He straightened slowly, every motion deliberate. Then he folded the letter with careful reverence and slipped it into the inside pocket of his cloak, near his heart.

When he spoke again, his voice was clearer. Still heavy—but steady.

"Why didn't you say anything last night?" he asked Corvina.

"You saw that chamber," she replied. "The shouting. The fear. No one was listening. If I had spoken then, the letter would have been drowned out in the noise. But now..."

She gestured quietly to the room. To the hush. To the sunrise glinting through the stained glass.

"Now the path is clear."

Alric nodded once.

He didn't feel ready. But perhaps that was the point.

He was no longer just a soldier. No longer only a friend to kings.

Now... he was something more.

Victor took a step back, then threw one arm across his chest and bowed with over-the-top flair. "So... do we all bow now, or...?"

The laughter that followed came easy, full, and real.

For the first time in days, it didn't sound like a defense.

It sounded like hope.

The morning came with a calm Marrathil had not known in weeks. The council reconvened—this time not with fire and fear, but with poise and purpose.

Lady Corvina opened the session with a clear voice and unwavering gaze. She presented King Thorim's final will and testament to the chamber, detailing the monarch's wishes. She reminded them of the precedent: in the event of a king's death with no heir, the council held authority to confirm the next ruler. Thorim had left no bloodline—but he had left something far stronger: trust.

The decision, once poised to erupt in argument and suspicion, now passed with unprecedented unity.

The council voted.

And for the first time in living memory, every voice echoed the same name.

King Alric.

Cheers erupted—not just within the council chamber, but from the corridors beyond, where word spread like wildfire. The Peacebound beamed with joy, tears in their eyes, for the first time in what felt like forever.

The coronation was unlike anything Marrathil had seen.

Banners of blue and gold rippled from every archway, and crowds filled every street and square. Bells rang from the tower. Trumpets echoed over the rooftops. What had been a city marked by suspicion and mourning now shimmered with celebration. After months of fear, and days teetering on the brink, Marrathil found release in revelry.

Alric stood before the gathered thousands in the great stone plaza, the rising sun painting the spires of the palace gold behind him. He was dressed in royal regalia now, though it felt strange on his broad shoulders. The circlet of kingship—simple but noble—was placed upon his brow, and the crowd erupted.

He raised a paw for silence, and the crowd hushed. His voice rang clear, strong, but warm.

"I was not born to be a king," Alric said. "I did not seek this crown. I have no noble lineage. I am only a servant of this city."

He paused, letting that settle.

"But perhaps that was exactly what Marrathil needed. Not a ruler who demands loyalty—but one who earns it. Not a voice that shouted above others—but one that listens. Not a throne of iron—but a heart of justice."

The crowd stood silent, leaning in on every word.

"We have walked through darkness. We have been lied to, betrayed, and broken. But here we were—still standing. Still together. And let it be known: Marrathil will remain a beacon. A light to the lost. A sanctuary of peace in a world that howls for war."

He turned slowly, looking out across the people.

"We will not let fear choose our path. We will not let division define us. We will hold fast to what makes us strong—our unity, our mercy, our truth. So long as I wear this crown, you will never walk alone."

A moment of silence followed—and then a thunderclap of cheers. Roars of joy shook the plaza. Flowers rained from balconies. Laughter and tears flowed freely.

The people of Marrathil had found their king.

And they loved him.

The echoes of celebration had faded, and the palace halls, once pulsing with music and mirth, now rested in quiet dignity. In a tall, sunlit chamber beyond the throne room, the Peacebound met with Alric once more—this time in private. Peanut noted the words carved into the marble stone wall, and realized how deeply they echoed everything the peacebound had witnessed in Marrathil.

"Shalonai rules what kings only pretend to."

Peanut, Kip, Victor, Malik, and Orin stood before King Alric, still dressed in the dust and road-wear of their long journey, a stark contrast to the polished marble beneath their feet.

Each of them offered a word of congratulations.

"You did it," said Orin with quiet pride.

"Well, now I have to act like I know what I'm doing," Alric said, a faint smile breaking the emotion on his face.

He looked at them, one by one.

"I owe you more than I can ever say," Alric said. "You didn't just help me... you saved this city. Saved me, perhaps more than once. If there's ever anything Marrathil—or I—can do for you, anything at all, do not hesitate to ask."

The Peacebound exchanged glances.

Peanut stepped forward.

"King Alric—"

He raised a paw.

"Just Alric, Peanut. I will always be just Alric to you five."

She gave a small nod. "Okay... Alric."

She took a breath.

"We came here on a mission, not just to protect Marrathil. We were the Peacebound, sent by Kazik. Our goal was to find the seven Kingstones, and one day forge the Crown of Ages—to choose a true king who can unite the lands of Avareth and bring lasting peace."

Alric blinked. "I... I've never heard of this. A Kingstone?"

Corvina, standing silently in the background until now, stepped forward.

"Sire," she said gently, "the Kingstone was just as they say. It was tradition—ancient, but true. The rightful king of each realm held their

Kingstone in trust. And in the forging of the Crown of Ages, it was the authority of each king to offer their stone in allegiance."

Alric turned toward her, stunned. "So... it's real? Marrathil had one?"

She nodded once. "Yes. And now, as king, it was your right to offer it."

Peanut's breath caught in her throat.

"But how would we even find it?" Alric asked.

Corvina said nothing. She simply raised a wing and pointed behind him.

Alric turned.

The room fell silent.

In the center of the great stained-glass window—newly repaired after the chaos of the past weeks—glimmered a radiant gem, blazing like captured sunlight.

The Kingstone.

Victor's jaw dropped.

Kip yelled, "You mean it's been right there this whole time? What were we even doing?!"

Orin gently placed a paw on Kip's shoulder. "The Kingstone cannot be taken," she reminded him. "It must be given. Only then did it carry meaning."

Kip muttered, "Still... would've been nice to know where it was."

They laughed softly, the tension melting.

Alric turned back to them and gave the order. Palace servants delicately brought down the gem, nestled in a cradle of velvet and gold.

He took it in his hands and stepped toward Peanut.

Then—he knelt.

With both arms extended, he held the Kingstone out before her.

"You have all shown yourselves to be worthy of royalty," he said solemnly. "The Kingstone of Marrathil was yours. Whomever you support as King of Avareth... Marrathil shall support as well. We will be your allies in this battle for peace."

Peanut reached out, her paws trembling.

She took it.

It didn't feel real.

When they left their home—when they stumbled through fire and betrayal, loss and sacrifice—this moment felt like a dream too far to touch. For a time, she had feared it would never come.

But here it was.

One Kingstone.

The first.

Alric rose to his feet.

The others gathered around her—Malik's eyes shining, Kip grinning ear to ear, Victor bouncing on his heels, and Orin, quiet and proud.

They had done it.

They did it.

And the journey was far from over.

But in that moment, they knew—

Peace could still win.

Epilogue

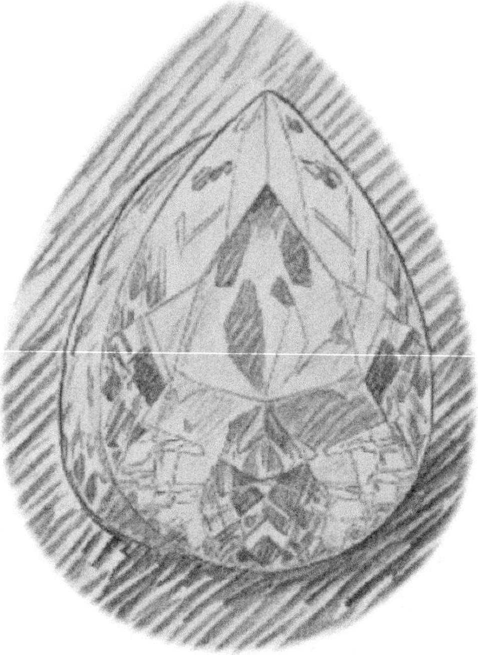

The sea stretched out in every direction—calm, endless, golden beneath the setting sun.

The Peacebound were going home.

After everything, Alric had insisted on offering an escort. Gilded boats, shining with polished brass and trimmed in rich purple and blue, bore them across the waves like honored ambassadors. The sails caught the wind like silk wings, and even the food was fresh and warm—cooked meals three times a day, soft blankets at night, music drifting on the breeze.

It felt like a vacation.

Nothing like the wild, creaking voyage on The Windrat, with its patchwork sails and mismatched crew. No crashing storms. No constant smell of fish. No risk of being thrown overboard by an angry turtle.

And yet, as Peanut stood at the bow, waves spraying her fur and the sun low on the horizon, she couldn't help but feel... nostalgic.

She could almost hear Polly squawking from the crow's nest. See Sump wheeling a mop bigger than he was. Feel the steady grumble of Mossback's voice echoing beneath the deck.

They had said their goodbyes—again—before setting off.

Mossback had been his usual gruff self, but there was something gentler in his voice as he clasped Peanut's paw one last time. Paul gave them each a carved bead made from the wood of the Windrat, and Sump had hugged Kip so hard he nearly popped.

Peanut had put in a good word for Mossback with Alric, who had been more than happy to offer the old pirate captain some well-paid work as a trusted seafarer. Mossback, to everyone's surprise, accepted it with a grunt that sounded suspiciously like gratitude.

Peanut missed them already.

"Third time's the charm, right?" she had said as they pulled away from the harbor.

Now, she leaned over the railing, watching the water rush beneath them. The wind tugged gently at her ears. The sky was on fire—streaked with orange, violet, and rose.

Footsteps padded behind her.

"...and then I told him," Kip's voice drifted up, already mid-story, "that's not a compass, that's his sandwich!"

Victor burst into laughter, nearly dropping the plum he'd been eating. Kip doubled over beside him, both of them gasping between chuckles as they reached her side.

Peanut couldn't help but smile.

"Glad to see you two haven't changed," she said, her voice warm.

"We've gotten worse, actually," said Victor, still giggling.

Kip leaned on the railing beside her. "You looked like you were thinking deep thoughts again. You okay?"

Peanut nodded, eyes still on the sunset. "Yeah... just remembering. I kind of miss the Windrat."

Kip wrinkled his nose. "Seriously? I still smell like fish guts from that boat."

Victor looked out over the horizon, letting the light catch in his golden fur. "I get it," he said. "That was where it all really began."

They stood in silence together, letting the sun sink slowly into the sea.

No one spoke for a while.

It wasn't the end of their journey—not even close. But for the first time in what felt like ages, there was no immediate danger. No looming betrayal. No fear.

Just the wind.

The water.

And hope.

"Do you think we'll actually do it?" Kip asked, his voice suddenly small. "Find all the stones? Finish the crown?"

Peanut looked at him, then at Victor. She felt the weight of the Kingstone in her pack, warm against her back like a promise.

"I don't know," she said honestly. "But I think we're going to try. Together."

Victor grinned. "That's good enough for me."

They stood there until the sun disappeared, leaving only stars and the sound of the sea.

Tomorrow, they would return to the Hollow.

But tonight... they just watched the sky.

Together.

Author's Note

Ashes of Peace is a fantasy tale, but it is deeply inspired by a real promise — one spoken on a mountainside over two thousand years ago:

"Blessed are the peacemakers, for they shall be called children of God."

Throughout these pages, you met creatures who long for peace but are caught in systems of fear, violence, and pride. That tension isn't just fiction — it's our world too. But I believe, with all my heart, that peace is possible. Not the kind built by might or ruled by fear, but the peace Shalonai brings: strong, true, and sacrificial.

If you saw glimpses of yourself in Peanut, Kip, Victor, or the Peacebound... good. You were meant to.

If you long for a kingdom where mercy wins, justice is real, and the true King returns — then keep reading. The journey is far from over.

Until then, may you walk the narrow road, carry light into the dark, and make peace in your corner of the world.

The true King is coming.

- K. G. Lyseng

Creator of all that was and is,

Bless the meek, the mourning, and the merciful.

Teach us to hunger for what is right,

And to make peace, not war.

Let our hands bring healing,

And our hearts stay pure.

We wait for the day Your promise is fulfilled

When the crown will return to the worthy,

Every tear be dried,

Every war be silenced.

For the true King is coming.

The story continues in Book 2 of the Peacebound Saga:

Paths of Mercy

Made in the USA
Las Vegas, NV
10 August 2025

26125647R00138